# THE RHETORICS OF
# POPULAR CULTURE

**Recent Titles in**
**Contributions to the Study of Popular Culture**

# The Rhetorics of Popular Culture

## ADVERTISING, ADVOCACY, AND ENTERTAINMENT

Robert L. Root, Jr.

CONTRIBUTIONS TO THE STUDY OF POPULAR CULTURE,
NUMBER 16

GREENWOOD PRESS
NEW YORK · WESTPORT, CONNECTICUT · LONDON

**Library of Congress Cataloging-in-Publication Data**

Root, Robert L.
  The rhetorics of popular culture.

  (Contributions to the study of popular culture,
ISSN 0198-9871 ; no. 16)
    Bibliography: p.
    Includes index.
      1. United States—Popular culture.  2. Rhetoric.
I. Title.  II. Series.
E169.12.R62    1987    808'.00141    86-14974
ISBN 0-313-24403-0 (lib. bdg. : alk. paper)

Library of Congress Catalog Card Number: 86-14974
ISBN: 0-313-24403-0
ISSN: 0198-9871

First published in 1987

Greenwood Press, Inc.
88 Post Road West, Westport, Connecticut 06881

Printed in the United States of America

∞

The paper used in this book complies with the
Permanent Paper Standard issued by the National
Information Standards Organization (Z39.48-1984).

10 9 8 7 6 5 4 3 2 1

For Caroline, my sunshine girl

# Contents

**Part IV.  Rhetoric and Entertainment**

# Figures

# Preface

The application of rhetorical analysis to popular culture is not original with me, but it has certainly been one of my professional preoccupations since becoming dissatisfied with traditional literary criticism as a means of exploring popular literature and discovering how rhetoric could provide a way to comprehend the interaction between the public and such forms of discourse as advertising, reviewing, science writing, popular music, and popular fiction. This book is an attempt to provide an overview of both popular culture and rhetoric and to demonstrate through analysis of individual forms of popular culture the ways they create their "rhetorics"—their communication with, and sometimes persuasion of, popular audiences.

The book has been a long time evolving and I am grateful for the encouragement its various elements received long before I knew that a book would eventually emerge from these varied interests. Some chapters began as guest lectures in the classes of colleagues at Central Michigan University, principally Ken Jurkiewicz, John Dinan, and Ron Primeau in English, Jim Walling in Speech, and Fred Branfon in Religion. I am grateful to them for allowing me the opportunity to develop the initial approach of this work in their classes.

Several chapters have also been presented in somewhat different form to meetings of the Michigan Council of Teachers of English, the Popular Culture and American Culture associa-

tions, and the MCTE/Michigan State University joint conference on teaching English. Chapter 6, "The Rhetoric of Reviewing," has been published in *The English Record*, and Chapter 9,
"A Listener's Guide to the Rhetoric of Popular Music," appeared in *The Journal of Popular Culture*. I am grateful to my
colleagues at these meetings for their interest and support.

My interest in and understanding of popular culture has been
encouraged as well by the responses to it of the children in my
life, Thomas Root, Caroline Root, and Rebecca Wildfong, who
have helped me to keep current in the changes it undergoes. I
thank them all with much love.

Finally, I have been nourished and enriched by the support
and interest of my wife, Sue, who has often helped me to a
better understanding of my own ideas in this book and has
always helped me to a better understanding of myself. I am
unable to measure my gratitude and love.

# Part I

# PRELIMINARIES

# 1

# The Nature of Popular Culture

While a general term like "popular culture" is used so often and so readily by such a wide range of people as to seem universal in its usage, even the casual reader of articles and books on the subject discerns a variety of definitions, either explicit or implied, for both parts of the term and disagreement about its boundaries, intentions, and contents. Such variety and such disagreement suggest at once the difficulties in exploring popular culture, but they also suggest ways of perceiving and understanding the underlying premises of any approach to the subject, because the ways critics define "popular culture" reveal the predispositions they bring to their examination of the subject and the limitations of their approaches.

For example, Dwight Macdonald has developed, over a period of years and through a cycle of similar articles, a "theory of mass culture" on hierarchical aesthetic grounds. In the opening sentences of his essay, "Masscult & Midcult," he writes:

For about two centuries Western culture has in fact been two cultures: the traditional kind—let us call it High Culture—that is chronicled in the textbooks, and a novel kind that is manufactured for the market. This latter may be called Mass Culture, or better Masscult, since it really isn't culture at all. Masscult is a parody of High Culture.[1]

We know at once several things about this author's perception that his "rhetoric"—the kind of persona he presents and the kind of attitude toward his subject and his audience he reveals through his use of language—makes clear beyond the presentation of his argument. One thing we understand is his approval of traditional culture—he identifies it as "traditional" and then prefers to extol it as "High Culture"—and his disapproval of Mass Culture—he denies that it is "culture" at all and coins a derogatory term for it, Masscult; throughout this long essay he will never shorten the term "High Culture" and never again stretch "Masscult" to its full length. A second thing we know is that this author intends to argue forcibly by subjective means. We feel at once the strength of his personal commitment and distaste. Finally, we should recognize that the author's predilection for High Culture and contempt for Mass Culture will continually lead him to bias his discussion.

In regard to this third point, notice particularly the inequity of his comparisons. The full range of "culture(s)" the article explores includes High Culture, Folk Art, Masscult, and Midcult, and the terms have little consistency. At one point he equates aesthetics with social class, High Culture being a product of the upper classes, Folk Art growing "mainly from below, an autochthonous product shaped by the people to fit their own needs."[2] The concept of Folk Art as "below" and High Culture as "high" should lead to a different nomenclature, High Culture and Low Culture, or Aristocratic Art and Folk Art, but to create that nomenclature would imply an equality in the parallelism which Macdonald doesn't want to suggest. Nor does he want to suggest that "Folk" create "culture"—that is the province of practitioners of High Culture alone in Macdonald's hierarchy.

The nomenclature for Masscult and Midcult is even more important to the author. Abbreviation eliminates the possibility that "culture" is being created here and "Mass," rather than "Popular," implies faceless anonymity and the loss of identity which comes from being part of the masses. The distinction is between "Folk" and "Mass," the first evocative of a certain class, the second evocative of mere bulk. But, again, the nomenclature is inconsistent: why isn't High Culture Individual Culture? Why aren't we classifying the three groups as Connoisseur, Professional, and Avocational Arts, if we are concerned with the relation of the artist to his creation and his class? Even Midcult, in Macdonald's terminology, is not between High Culture and Folk Culture, but between High Culture and Masscult. That is, it is not the middle of two respectable cultures, but the middle between the *only* respectable culture and a non-culture preferable to Midcult itself.

Macdonald's biases abound throughout his essay. Calling High Culture traditional implies that folk culture isn't, when in fact on some levels it is *more* traditional than Highcult. Stating that High Culture is found in textbooks and not in the market is erroneous; the highest of Highcult figures, William Shakespeare, was a quintessential literary entrepreneur. To call Masscult novel, as if novelty were perjorative, and then to extol the avant-garde, which is *expressly* non-traditional, as Macdonald does later in the article, is to confuse them utterly. Smelling out Midcult works of Highcult authors (Hemingway's *Old Man and the Sea* is Midcult, *The Sun Also Rises* Highcult) or Midcult *sections* of Highcult works is to take these confusing distinctions to idiosyncratic extremes.

One could easily go through the whole of Macdonald's mass culture theorizing and cite example after example of inconsistency and subjectivity, but the point should be clear that his approach is based on predispositions he has toward class and aesthetic artifacts. His theory of mass culture grows out of those predispositions rather than out of an objective examination of artifacts and a clearly defined set of terms (Is Macdonald saying that "folk" don't have a culture?). As Bernard Rosenberg makes clear, Macdonald's position is really more connected with his politics, particularly his reaction to modern media, what Rosenberg calls "machine civilization." Rosenberg sees a close tie between political position and reaction to popular culture:

The political lines that have crystalized are approximately these: radicals (Dwight Macdonald, Clement Greenberg, Irving Howe) who, like the arch-conservatives (Ortega y Gasset, T. S. Eliot, Bernard Iddings Bell), although for opposite reasons, are repelled by what they commonly regard as vulgar and exploitive, and the liberals (Gilbert Seldes, David Reisman, Max Lerner) who take a predictable position in the middle. The parallel between left, right, and center in politics and on the 'popular arts' is virtually perfect.[3]

That is, radicals see popular culture as exploitive of the lower classes, conservatives see popular culture as debased and menacing, and liberals see all culture and all classes as equally valid and valuable. However one views this question, it is chiefly one which equates politics with aesthetics, and worries less about what popular culture is than about what motives lie behind it and how it effects "high culture."

To further understand the relationship between definition and disposition, examine a separate interpretation of what popular culture is. In the preface to *The Unembarrassed Muse*, Russel Nye attempts to make very clear what he means by "popular arts":

*Popular* is interpreted to mean "generally dispersed and approved"— descriptive of those artistic productions which express the taste and understanding of the majority and which are free of control in context and execution from minority standards of correctness. The *arts*, as the term is used in this study, are works in literature, music, drama, and other artistic and broadly human forms, produced for and expressive of the convictions, tastes, values, and feelings of the general public: intended, that is, for mass consumption.[4]

Nye, like Macdonald and most other writers on the subject, acknowledges the two artistic traditions of the learned and unlettered classes prior to the rise of the middle class in the mid-eighteenth century and attributes the growth of the popular arts to the growth of an audience prepared for it and a technology able to provide it. Nye's breakdown of the three artistic traditions into folk art, popular art, and elite art is cognizant of distinctions among the artists, their attitudes toward their art and their audience, the disparate natures of their audiences, and the means of distribution, without assigning greater value to any one of them and without mixing intentions. He is also less concerned with exclusivity than critics like Macdonald, who worry greatly about pedigree and contamination of superior categories by inferior categories. Although Nye's terms seem similar to Macdonald's, they are in fact more consistent with one another—the nomenclature identifies the same characteristics of all traditions rather than unique characteristics of each tradition—and, more importantly, the relationships among them are immediately clear. Finally, Nye's categories are not, like

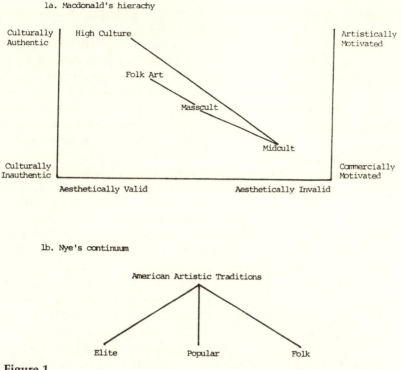

Figure 1.
**Two Representations of the Relationships among Artistic Traditions**

Macdonald's, arranged hierarchically or qualitatively, but rather continuously—that is, on a continuum, where each has equal value (Figure 1).

Obviously, as a reader, I find Nye's arrangement more convincing and reliable than Macdonald's. It seems to me more objectively analytical and bias-free; Nye's book is a historical overview of popular arts in America and seems at the outset to be less judgmental about them; that is, it neither devalues them nor overvalues them. My reaction is also a response to his rhetoric. He presents himself as a careful, reasonable man—defining terms at the outset, clarifying relationships, examining rather than, as in Macdonald's case, denouncing—and I respond favorably to that presentation because it allows me more room to exercise my own judgment rather than simply to react to the writer's attempts to persuade me of his judgment.

But Nye's arrangement is convincing and reliable to me also because of the predispositions I bring to the examination of popular culture, including a tendency to arrange categories and subcategories systematically and continuously, rather than hierarchically, and a belief that categories of a single subject ought to be approached with consistency and openmindedness. Not the least portion of my compatibility with Nye's position is the background I bring to his discussion of it.

Just as Macdonald brings a political/aesthetic perspective to his analysis, and Nye brings a historical perspective, each of us brings to each experience a particular approach. For example, a group of people seeing the same film may respond differently (and usually do). My response to Bob Fosse's *All That Jazz* was to be profoundly moved and emotionally drained by the experience, but some critics attacked it for its autobiographical elements, others for its aesthetic kinship to a Fellini film, and still others for its stylized presentation. In effect, responses to the film were often particular to the individual viewer, even though the critics nominally share an aesthetic sense about the film. An examination of the reviews of virtually any film will demonstrate the intermingling of subjective and objective responses.

For most people most of the time, the confusion of subjective and objective reactions, of taste and judgment, is not a significant dilemma. Most of us are not significantly engaged in the analysis of art and culture, and our responses to them on a personal level allow us to take from them what we individually need and disregard, or at least accept uncritically, the rest. But, when we are engaged in the analysis of art and culture, we need to be very clear about the relationship of our individual taste and our judgment, to know well the predispositions we bring to such an analysis and the system under which we conduct it. That system ought to be consistent, flexible, and objective.

Culture is a rather vague term that we use freely and without clear referents. To talk of Western culture, American culture, or popular culture is to refer sweepingly to elements of human society which may not be implicitly agreed upon by everyone who uses those terms. For my purposes, "culture" is all those activities and artifacts which make up the intellectual and social components of a civilization or society, including its arts, technology, commerce, politics, and divertissements. Such a definition may seem all encompassing and I mean it to be, because culture is all encompassing. Attempts to distinguish among categories of culture on a basis of class are increasingly irrelevant, except on a historical basis. Even then, lines of demarcation are not always clear: Shakespeare wrote for groundlings as well as courtiers, and a play like Ben Jonson's *Bartholomew Fair* assumes commerce with the most common aspects of Jacobean life on the part of the most elite audiences.

Class distinctions in culture are misleading because they argue a uniqueness for each category that they may not actually have. While acknowledging that a creator is very "independent of his time and place; the demands of the audience have always largely determined his work," Macdonald goes on to claim that

before 1750, these demands were themselves disciplined by certain standards of excellence which were accepted by both the limited public of informed amateurs and the artists who performed for them. Today, in the United States, the demands of the audience, which has changed from a small body of connoisseurs into a large body of ignoramuses, have become the chief criteria of success.[5]

"The question," he asserts, "was not how good the work is but how popular it will be." There are two confusions in this position. The first is that "good" and "popular" are antithetical—Shakespeare, Moliere, and Dickens wrote for popular audiences, and their work is widely acclaimed by connoisseurs. The second is that there is a universal qualitative difference between the judgment of "connoisseurs" and the judgment of "ignoramuses" (what Macdonald elsewhere terms the "cognoscenti" and the "ignoscenti"). Granting him the view that his distinction is not perjorative but merely meant to indicate the differences between those specially learned in a field and those unschooled in the same field, we still need not grant that one field is qualitatively superior to another or that connoisseurs in one field are not ignoramuses in others. The full appreciation of the fine points of bullfighting, boxing, tennis, or football may demand certain familiarity and specialized knowledge—the aficionado is usually more sophisticated than the novice—but such sophistication on the part of boxing cognoscenti does not confer on boxing superiority over tennis, or vice versa.

Such distinctions also ignore a universality of response which transcends dilettantism and aestheticism. That is, narrative, dramatic, and lyric literature demands certain responses from readers, viewers, and listeners regardless of the intellectual intentions and abilities of their creators and audiences. What makes *King Lear* an enduring and meaningful work is its portrayal of certain aspects of the human condition which can be received and experienced by any viewer regardless of the degree of specialized knowledge he has about Jacobean theater, the conventions of tragedy, Shakespeare's *oeuvre*, or English history.

Thus, while I might acknowledge that appreciation or even comprehension of certain cultural experiences demands specialized knowledge and background—for example, opera, French Neo-Classical drama, modern Metafiction—I want to claim that there are elements of cultural experience which are universal and illimitable by class distinctions. Elite art, popular art, and folk art communicate in the same ways, though not always by the same means, and though we can make distinctions among artists, art forms, audiences, and treatment of subject matter, the universality of those components in art is more significant than arguable distinctions of aesthetic value.

In principle, then, I agree with Russel Nye's definition of the popular arts. In particular I want to define popular culture as those activities and artifacts among the intellectual and social components of a civilization or society which are "generally dispersed and approved," "produced for, and expressive of the convictions, tastes, values, and feelings of the general public; intended, that is, for mere consumption," "accessible intellectually and logistically to the broadest spectrum of the society." Again, I am being encompassing—in a democratic society almost all aspects of the culture are logistically accessible—and I have no intention of drawing clear boundaries between popular and non-popular (unpopular ?) culture, largely because I'm not certain what they are, and also because I am certain that much of what I will be saying in the following chapters about certain categories of popular culture is applicable as well to equivalent categories of "elite culture" and "folk culture" as well.

To better understand the nature of American popular culture we will need to examine some of its artifacts closely. The artifacts of any culture are related to three areas: entertainment, commerce, and information. That is, artifacts will exemplify a society's interest in amusing itself, in providing goods and services for itself, and in informing itself about its activites, including events which are of interest and significance to its community and also ideas about itself and its members' relationships with other cultures and one another. Although activities and artifacts may embody much more, communication is a central element of entertainment, commerce, and information. The ways in which these categories order communication are vital to an understanding of popular culture, indeed, of any culture.

Entertainment may embody activities devoid of intellectual content, but most entertainment, particularly that involving the arts, in fact communicates values and concepts. All artistic aspects of culture are value laden, sometimes despite themselves, and the ways in which they communicate merit attention. Commerce, which may include a whole range of non-verbal artifacts—the products which make up the merchandise of our commercial life—also embodies communications of values and concepts in the advertising that sells these products. Information is dispensed through various means and media of communication, but little if any information is dispensed value-free; every piece of reporting and "objective" observing is in fact highly value laden. A large part of the information dispensed in any culture is also chiefly advocacy of certain values and certain convictions. Advocacy is everywhere—in newspaper columns on an incredible range of subjects, in self-help and popular/academic books and articles, in evaluative reviews of virtually every product, including art.

The communication aspects of the major branches of culture have in common the fact that they do communicate, that they contain and often espouse or convey specific values and opinions, and that they can be usefully and valuably examined by the same principles of analysis that we apply to all other areas of discourse, the principles of rhetorical analysis. In advertising, for example, the attempts at persuasion may be uniform in purpose—the desire to sell a product or service—but the kinds of advertising are varied and their rhetorical devices increasingly complex and sophisticated as they move from such advertising as direct mail (a primary rhetorical situation, the verbal pitch), to print advertising (the visual pitch), to television commercials (the video pitch). Advocacy is more sophisticated than advertising in the sense that it makes more demands on the audience to understand the argument and to evaluate its separate points; it varies from the relatively expository espousing of scientific values to the evaluative expression of artistic values (as in criticism or reviewing) to the full-fledged persuasive writing of national political columnists. Entertainment might seem on the surface to be non-rhetorical, but in fact the discourse which occurs in entertainment is merely embodied in less direct expression, and the elements of discourse are as much a primary basis for entertainment as for any other means of communication. Popular music and television programs imply, if not express, specific values; popular genres of fiction are built upon implicit relationships between the artist, the audience, and the subject.

Advertising, advocacy, and entertainment are thus aspects of popular culture especially appropriate for rhetorical analysis, and the major portion of this book will be given to explicit rhetorical analysis of these forms of communication. However, before that can be done, we need to establish a context for the principles of rhetorical analysis.

# 2

# The Elements of Rhetoric

Popular culture, in the sense we have defined it in Chapter 1, is a modern phenomenon, only a few centuries old. Rhetoric, on the other hand, is as old as culture itself. The earliest literary artifacts of any number of cultures contain examples of explicitly rhetorical acts, and since these works are usually transcriptions of epic material which circulated orally for generations before they were written down, it seems obvious that rhetoric is as old as communication. The fact that speeches and acts of persuasion are recorded in works like *The Iliad* and *The Odyssey*, *Beowulf* and *The Epic of Gilgamesh* not only establishes the great age of rhetoric but also its vital place in literature. Rhetoric is thus essential to human communication and essential as well to literary expression.

But rhetoric, like popular culture, is an elusive term and used in a variety of ways that are often contradictory and confusing. In this chapter, I intend to clarify the meaning of rhetoric in my own terms and the applications to which it may be put in analysis of cultural artifacts.

Edward P. J. Corbett defines rhetoric this way: "Rhetoric is the art or the discipline that deals with the use of discourse, either spoken or written, to inform or persuade or move an audience, whether that audience is made up of a single person or a group of persons."[1] As he observes, this is a broad definition, seeming to take in all discourse, but at its heart rhetoric is exactly that sweeping. The classical definition of rhetoric was Aristotle's and seems at the outset to be more limited; he defined it as "the faculty of discovering in the particular case what are the available means of persuasion."[2] Corbett argues for a broad interpretation of Aristotle's definition:

When one is reminded that the Greek word for *persuasion* derives from the Greek verb "to believe," one sees that Aristotle's definition can be made to comprehend not only those modes of discourse which are "argumentative" but also those "expository" modes of discourse which seek to win acceptance of information or explanation.[3]

Corbett's broader view is surely more accurate a description of rhetoric in practice. Although a good deal of the history of rhetorical study has been centered on the making and critiquing of persuasive speeches—the explicit focus of rhetoric—a few minutes analysis of other literary forms reveal the rhetorical aspects of "non-argumentative" literature as well. Aristotle's *Rhetoric* is an attempt to analyze rhetoric, to explain what it is and how it works, but it is also a defense of rhetoric against charges of immorality and irresponsibility. Plato, Aristotle's teacher, had attacked rhetoric in two famous dialogues, the *Gorgias* and the *Phaedrus*, charging that it trained young people to argue convincingly regardless of the truth behind their arguments. Plato took the view that dialectic, a common effort by well-meaning people to examine a subject and arrive at the truth about it, was preferable to rhetoric, an attempt by a single person to define the truth and persuade others to accept his position. His case was influential enough to make Aristotle open his own book on rhetoric with the sentence, "Rhetoric is the counterpoint of dialectic," and assert that "everybody to some extent makes use of both Dialectic and Rhetoric; for all make some attempt to sift or support theses, and to defend or attack persons."[4]

To some extent the argument is irresolvable: the same tricks of rhetoric can be used to persuade people of the false as readily as of the true, and yet those who somehow arrive at the truth without having the means to convince others of it are likely to be ineffective. When modern writers and speakers criticize others for their "empty rhetoric" or "mere rhetoric," they in fact see rhetoric simply as a series of maneuvers in communication which attempt to persuade without benefit of an honest motive or valid argument. But of course those writers and speakers, in trying to persuade us of the emptiness or untrustworthiness of another's position, are using rhetoric themselves.

In the same way, Plato's dialogues, while they attempt to model the dialectical approach, are simultaneously rhetorical, both within the speeches that make up the dialogue and in the structure of the dialogue itself. Modern students frequently bristle at the character of Socrates who so often seems less to be engaging in dialectical attempts to find the truth than to lead his fellow speakers through a dialectical process to a position that Socrates himself has already reached. Socrates' curiosity and sincerity seem feigned, an attempt to avoid making the other speaker take an adversarial position. Of course, this *is* what happens in the dialogues because Plato wrote them to persuade readers of the positions that Socrates and his fellow speakers will arrive at by the end; the pattern of the dialogue is structured to lead to that conclusion. It is persuasive writing, rhetorical writing, although the argument takes the form of a dialogue rather than a speech. The rhetorical act occurs both in the speeches of the characters as they attempt to argue back and forth and in the dialogue in general as Plato attempts to use it to convince his readers.

While Aristotle confines the practice of rhetoric to three kinds of speeches—deliberative or legislative, those that persuade or dissuade; forensic or judicial, those that accuse or defend; and epideictic or ceremonial, those that praise or blame[5]—the fact that he defends rhetoric at the same time that he purports simply to be explaining it or analyzing it reveals that he himself is engaging in rhetorical practice beyond the scope of his own definition. Thus the evidence of the work of Plato and Aristotle themselves demonstrates that rhetoric takes in not only public oratory and written argument but also expository works like Aristotle's *Rhetoric* and literary works like the dialogues or philosophic dramas of Plato. Any discourse has a rhetorical basis.

The most common model of discourse is the communication

triangle (Figure 2). As Kinneavy describes it, "basic to all uses of language are a person who encodes a message, the signal (language) which carries the message, the reality to which the message refers, and the decoder (receiver of the message)."[6] He also points out that these terms vary in different fields—a literary theorist talks of the artist, the audience, the object, and the universe; the communications theorist of speaker, listener, speech, and subject; the semanticist of expressor, receptor, referend, and referent—but the structure itself, which originates in Aristotle's *Rhetoric*, is commonly accepted as a viable model of discourse.[7]

We can apply this model to the areas of popular culture we will be examining in this book. The discourse of advertising consists of the interaction of advertiser (entrepreneur/salesman) and customer/client concerning a product or service through the means of advertising (commercial, print ad); the discourse of entertainment consists of an artist or artists performing for an audience (readers, listeners, viewers) concerning the expression of feeling or opinion about a subject through performance (book, song, theater); the discourse of advocacy consists of a speaker or writer addressing an audience concerning an opinion through a speech or a text (column, editorial, review, article, book) (Figure 3).

Kinneavy has pointed out "how thoroughly this triangle pervades the structure of the *Rhetoric*."[8] For example, Aristotle argues that there are three kinds of rhetorical proof; that is, three ways in which a speaker can persuade an audience of his position—ethos, pathos, and logos.[9] *Ethos* is ethical proof, the convincing character of the speaker. Aristotle says that "the character of the speaker is a cause for persuasion when the speech is so uttered as to make him worthy of belief" and points out that "on points outside the realm of exact knowledge, where opinion is divided we trust ['men of probity'] absolutely." While he argues that this trust should be created by the speech itself, he affirms that the speaker's "character is the most potent of all the means of persuasion."[10] In a larger sense, beyond the view of the speaker as simply a persuader, we can see that in any discourse the personality of the speaker may have a greater affect on his audience than other factors—a Frank Sinatra, for

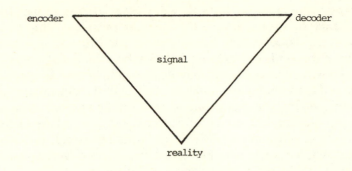

**Figure 2.**
**The Communication Triangle**

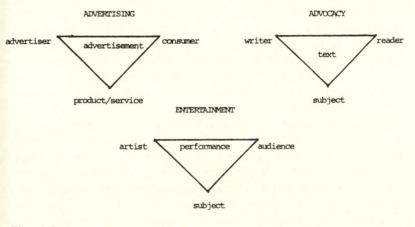

**Figure 3.**
**The Discourse of Popular Culture**

example, may be more attractive because of his on-stage persona than because of the subject of his songs.

*Pathos* is an appeal to the emotions of the audience. Observes
Aristotle, "We give very different decisions under the sway of
pain or joy, and liking or hatred."[11] To be able to effectively
use an emotional appeal, the speaker must have a sense of his

audience, and audience appeals will vary according to the class of listener or reader whom the speaker perceives himself as addressing. For Aristotle this discussion led to a long examination of the kinds of emotions that may be most readily aroused and the ways that speakers may legitimately arouse them—the abuses of the emotional appeal, as well as of the ethical appeal, are obvious, but the rhetorician from Aristotle onward assumes that the speaker will not be untruthful and that to be effective he needs to have control over both kinds of appeal, for these appeals will be made whether he intends them or not and may be counterproductive if not controlled properly.

The third kind of rhetorical proof, *logos*, is logical proof, or argument, the kind of proof that appeals to reason. Aristotle knew that such a proof is the most reliable, the most legitimate in terms of truthfulness, because it is the one most overtly argumentative. Logical proof involves the presentation of the subject or the argument—its arrangement, its use of evidence, its validity in relation to its circumstances and essential elements. Like the other kinds of proof, it too is subject to abuse, particularly to fallacious arguments, whether from faulty reasoning or from deceptive presentation of evidence.

It is essential to recognize that ethos, pathos, and logos are part of every discourse; they exist as dimensions of the elements of the communication triangle (speaker, listener, subject) as well as in the perceptions of the discourse by those involved in it (the speaker's view of himself, his subject, and his audience; the listener's view of his speaker, the presentation of the subject, and himself as audience). Thus, while we might be able to separate and analyze each of these elements as parts of the discourse situation overall, we are also able to analyze them collectively in regard to each separate part of the communication triangle.

Moreover, our sense of these elements will change according to at least two other primary factors, which are tightly related and which have to do with the nature of the specific discourse. Aristotle's breakdown of the kinds of rhetoric into legislative, judicial, and ceremonial is an acknowledgment that the *aim* of the discourse will determine the form in which it is expressed.

In terms of discourse generally, modern theorists have recognized broader categories. Kinneavy's model is widely ac-

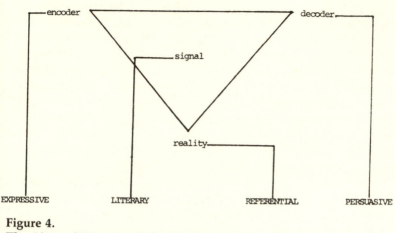

**Figure 4.**
**The Aims of Discourse (after Kinneavy)**

cepted. He divides the aims of discourse into expressive, literary, referential, and persuasive categories, each according to its
primary purpose.[12] In expressive writing, for example, the writer
is chiefly concerned with exploring and expressing personal
views and feelings; in literary discourse the writer's attention
is on the form of the written product; in referential (or expository) discourse the writer is chiefly concerned to make the subject clear; in persuasive (or argumentative) discourse the writer
is primarily interested in convincing an audience or changing
their position.[13] Accordingly, Kinneavy connects the aims of
discourse with elements on the communication triangle (Figure
4).[14]

This orientation or primary attention never negates the other
elements—all are present in every discourse—but it does suggest ways of distinguishing among varieties of discourse. In
the discourse of popular culture, for example, communication
in entertainment may have a chiefly literary function; its attention is very often on the form of the discourse, the kind of
artifact it is, the genre to which it belongs. A film by Brian de
Palma, for example, is chiefly an imitation of, and possibly
homage to, the films of Alfred Hitchcock; however commercial
the intentions of either producer or director, the primary emphasis of a film like *Dressed to Kill* or *Blow-Out* is on distinctive

elements of its form. The same is true of television programs, popular songs, and popular fiction, particularly that which is chiefly identified as generic (mystery, romance, Gothic, western). Communication in advertising is chiefly persuasive, obviously; it attempts to convince an audience to buy a product or make use of a service. In works of advocacy the aim may be expressive (observations, personal reminiscences), referential (textbooks, reviews, reportage), or persuasive (editorials, political columns, criticism). The aim of the discourse will determine much about the nature of its elements of proof (its ethos, pathos, and logos).

Another vital aspect of the rhetoric of any popular culture is *mode*. Entertainment, advertising, and advocacy are all aims of popular discourse; film, television, direct mail, television commercials, editorials, and reviews are all modes of discourse. Having accepted or chosen a specific mode to work in, a writer needs to observe certain conventions which serve as restraints on his rhetorical design. Moreover, within certain modes are subcategories which further influence design—a mystery demands certain elements that would be out of place in a supernatural horror story; radio demands certain conventions that television does not; a movie review is a different kind of artifact than an editorial. In part this is a question of definition—a reviewer like Arthur Schlesinger does a great deal of editorializing in his reviews—but it is also a question of expectation. It is related to the ways the "encoder" sees himself, his subject, and his audience, and the ways his "decoder" responds to his ethos and his presentation of the subject.

These are universal elements of the rhetoric of discourse: ethos, pathos, logos, aim, and mode. They are as applicable to elite culture as to folk culture or popular culture. Not only is the way an Emily Dickinson presents her view of reality different from the way a Robert Frost does, but their personas (the ethos presented in their poetry) are radically different as well; not only is the audience for Rudyard Kipling's work different from the audience for W. H. Auden's, but their aims are different as well; not only is the aim of Horace's poetry different from the aim of Ovid's but the modes are as well—to write elegies or sonnets or haiku or odes effects the outcome of the artifact.

The analysis of the rhetorics of popular culture in this book will be based on these five elements. In every case I will attempt to apply rhetorical analysis to a specific aspect of popular culture and repeatedly ask the same questions about them: What is the mode of presentation? How does the mode affect the presentation? What is the purpose of the discourse? How is the discourse arranged to achieve that purpose? Who is the audience for the discourse? How is the discourse directed at that audience? What is the ethos of the discourse? What persona is created, how is it created, and why is it created? What is the argument of the discourse? How is it arranged? Upon what is it based? Generally these are questions of rhetoric which can be asked of any discourse.

In addition to demonstrating how rhetorical analysis can illuminate various aspects of popular culture, the book will also argue for the importance of seeing such aspects as discourse. In an area like advertising, where a body of rhetorical study has appeared, this may not seem new, but in certain other areas of popular culture the rhetorical approach has either been overlooked or misapplied in the past.

To take one area not examined in the book, film, we can see the confusion that arises from an attempt to create rigid hierarchies within a mode of discourse by examining O. B. Hardison's comments on Alfred Hitchcock as a rhetorician. While referring to Hitchcock as "one of the great professionals in the movie business—probably the greatest" Hardison carefully selects his words, because he is really going to attempt to devalue Hitchcock's work in the article by placing it in the category of rhetoric and reserving the category of art for other filmmakers. As he writes:

Nobody would seriously compare Hitchcock to a dozen directors and producers who have used the film medium as an art form. Eisenstein, Chaplin, Ford, Bergman, Olivier, Fellini—the list could be expanded.

He goes on to make the following distinction:

Consider the professional a rhetorician. The purpose of art, says Aristotle, is to give pleasure. Not any kind of pleasure, but the sort that comes from learning. The experience of art is an insight, an illumination of the action being imitated. Rhetoric, on the other hand, is oriented toward the marketplace. Its purpose is not illumination but persuasion, and its governing concept is that the work produced must be adjusted to the mind of the audience.[15]

Hardison concludes, "We study a work of art aesthetically, but the study of professional entertainment is a branch of sociology."

Such a distinction between art and rhetoric is capricious, reminiscent of the same kind of elitist categorizing that Dwight Macdonald was seen to engage in in Chapter 1. Aristotle himself, to cite Hardison's own authority, referred in his treatise on literary art to its kinship with rhetoric:

As for the Thought, we may assume what is said of it in our Art of Rhetoric, as it belongs more properly to that department of inquiry.[16]

In Aristotle's view poetics and rhetorics are two divisions of discourse which overlap and which have no inherent superiority to one another. Examining the same issues in this century, Hoyt H. Hudson concluded:

I have tried to emphasize the distinction between pure poetry and rhetoric, and then to suggest that rarely do we find them pure; that poetry in some of its most usual forms is more or less strongly tinged with a rhetorical element; that criticism will walk with surer feet if it can learn to isolate and analyze this rhetorical element.[17]

By poetry both Aristotle and Hudson are encompassing the whole of artistic discourse.

We need only to examine the very filmmakers that Hardison sets apart from "professionals" like Hitchcock to confirm the validity of Hudson's remarks. Eisenstein, at the head of that list, is best remembered for such films as *Potemkin*, *October*, and *Alexander Nevsky*, the first two commemorations of the Russian Revolution, the third a stirring work of anti-German propaganda. Chaplin's *Modern Times* and *The Great Dictator* are also works with a specific point of view which all elements in the films reinforce. Whatever else these works of art may be, they are overwhelmingly rhetorical. Moreover, all of the filmmakers

on Hardison's list are surely professionals, not merely dilet-
tantes and surely not amateurs, the terms we presume to be
the antithesis of the professional.

To some extent the problem with Hardison's analysis of
Hitchcock is not his attempt to make distinctions among filmmakers but rather the imprecision and inaccuracy of his terminology and the bias of his evaluation. If we are to have more
balanced, better informed analysis of the artifacts of culture,
we will need to become more aware of the universality of discourse and the ways in which rhetoric is inherent in all the
ways human beings communicate with one another. Modern
discourse theory has become increasingly aware of this universality. Marie Hochmuth Nichols writes of Kenneth Burke:

one might say that Burke would bring within the scope of rhetoric
any and all symbolic resources that function to promote social cohesion, and all symbolic resources that induce attitude or action. Now
this is not to say that a book on mathematics could just as well be
thought of as a book on rhetoric. But it does say that to the extent
that a book on mathematics has meaning, it is a preparation for action,
hence has a rhetorical ingredient in it. . . . . It says that when the an-
thropologist concerns himself with the use of magic as a means of
promoting social cohesion in early tribal groups, he has entered the
rhetorical field, or when the social psychologist studies the cohesiveness of a society and the means by which this cohesiveness is imple-
mented, he is examining rhetorical matters. It means that when the
poet or the playwright, or the short story writer, or speaker is manip-
ulating symbols to the end of inducing an attitude in the reader, or to
make the reader say, "How moving," he is making language perform
a rhetorical function.[18]

As Burke himself writes, "We can place in terms of rhetoric all
those statements by anthropologists, ethnologists, individual and
social psychologists, and the like that bear upon the *persuasive*
aspects of language, the function of language as *addressed*, as
direct or roundabout appeal to real or ideal audiences, without
or within."[19]

James Kinneavy hints at the breadth of rhetorical application
in a recent overview of research by listing the areas he *cannot*
explore in his essay:

I will not consider some of the following very legitimate areas of rhetoric: marketing, managerial rhetoric, discussion and debating techniques, interviewing, oral interpretation, film and radio and television production (as such), literary theory and criticism, linguistics, general semantics and modern linguistic semantics, narrative theory, theory of description, axiology, logic, and the philosophy of science.[20]

Such a range of potential applications suggests the significance of rhetorical analysis for an understanding of not only forms of discourse but also the essential ingredients of a culture. In the following chapters we will attempt to demonstrate its utility in some of our culture's more prominent modes of discourse.

# Part II

# RHETORIC AND ADVERTISING

# 3

# The Rhetoric of Direct Mail: The Verbal Pitch

To begin analyzing the rhetorics of popular culture, we turn first to advertising, because it is the most available, the most accessible and the simplest in terms of what it hopes to accomplish. Primarily, advertising attempts to persuade consumers to purchase a product or service. The simplest ad hopes merely for identification—the consumer's recognition of a specific product when confronted with a choice in the supermarket—and can consist of merely a logo or trademark emblazoned on a sweatshirt, cap, or bumper sticker. In this section of the book we will look at three forms of advertising—direct mail, print advertising, and television commercials—tracing a course through increasingly sophisticated media and examining the ways modern media presents rhetorical elements constant in all forms of advertising.

As an example of discourse and a model of the rhetorical situation, direct mail advertising is as traditional, uncomplicated, and overt as any area of popular communication. Direct mail—the junk mail that arrives at our homes weekly, if not daily—exemplifies rhetoric working in very traditional ways: a speaker (an advertiser) addressing an audience (a customer) about the subject (the product or service) in a direct address (letter of solicitation) for a specific purpose (to sell the product or service). It is therefore an especially useful place to begin analyzing the rhetorics of popular culture.

The purpose of direct mail advertising is obvious—the ultimate goal of all advertising is to sell the consumer on the thing advertised; it is a persuasive act which in direct mail is performed almost as directly and overtly as a political address. Other forms of advertising, particularly print advertising and television commercials, which we will analyze in later chapters, persuade in images or actions as well as in words, but direct mail advertising has to rely largely on language; the colorful brochures and fliers which accompany the advertiser's letter may enhance it, but they don't necessarily carry the primary force of the persuasion. The purpose of the advertising is achieved when the reader returns the prepaid postcard or subscription form or application.

The mode of direct mail advertising is chiefly that of correspondence, an epistolary discourse between two people. The interest in promoting that sense of communication is so strong that some advertisers program individual names and addresses and references into the form letters, to give the illusion of greater personal interest. Because direct mail advertising imitates the form of correspondence, its visual representation as a communication act is that of the communication triangle with the terms "encoder, decoder, reality, signal" replaced by "advertiser, customer, product, letter." Unlike other modes of advertising, direct mail creates the illusion of direct communication, even at its most impersonal, because of the conventions of correspondence, and part of its persuasive force is the sense of obligation it creates in the reader to reply, an obligation that print and television advertising do not engender.

Advertising is a rhetorical act because it involves a persuader's attempt to convince someone through the three means of rhetorical persuasion, *ethos*, *pathos*, and *logos*. The persuader has to create a persona within the correspondence; even the attempt to avoid creating a persona does in fact create one. An announcer on television or radio may be interested chiefly in conveying the sense of the words he reads aloud, but tone, inflection, intonation, speed, volume, and other factors convey a sense of the speaker as well. In fact, announcers are especially chosen for the ethos they convey through their voices;

this is why people like Don Pardo, Bill Wendell, and Johnny Olson announce game shows and not programs like *Nova* or *National Geographic*, as actors like Alexander Scourby or Richard Basehart do. Style, vocabulary, syntax, and other language elements create cues to personas in written discourse, even the most impersonal. But in works which are admittedly persuasive in aim, no attempt is made to eschew ethical proof; as we shall see, it may often be the chief focus of the persuasion.

The persuader also has to have a sense of whom his audience is and how to appeal to that audience. Individual advertisers don't attempt to persuade everyone; a general appeal to buy a specific product would be a waste of energy and perhaps more importantly, of advertising dollars. In fact, advertising in every mode is usually targeted at a specific audience which is well defined before the advertising is created and is also usually clearly identified in the advertisements themselves. The advertiser's job is to know to whom he intends to sell and to make that potential buyer respond positively to the product by appealing to some specific emotion or interest in that buyer. Direct mail advertising is often directed at consumers who have been identified as potential buyers because of their current status or their previously expressed interests. For example, the consumer who subscribes to *National Geographic* will inevitably find himself solicited by publishers of competing or parallel publications like the *Smithsonian Magazine*, *Geo*, *Audubon*, and *Nature*; a subscriber to a magazine like *Saturday Review* may end up on the mailing list of *Atlantic*, *Harper's*, *New York Review of Books*, and others. Companies sell their subscription lists to other companies, and audiences are defined and delineated by the evidence of previous interest. Naturally, individual consumers are more varied and eclectic in their tastes than advertisers take them to be, but, in terms of reaching a target audience, advertisers are more successful limiting the potential audience and representing it narrowly in the advertising.

The direct mail letter is usually designed to present an argument of some kind, something that appeals to the reader's reason. Unlike other forms of advertising, where the argument is implicit or non-existant, the direct mail letter, by virtue of its reliance on prose, has to build some sort of logos, although these arguments are seldom fully articulated. One sense of the argumentative is in the post-script to many direct mail letters where a figure other than the signatory of the full letter asks the consumer why he or she has decided not to respond to the offer. Perhaps the letter has promised one free issue of a magazine and no further issues until specifically ordered; the post-script wants to know why the consumer would turn down an opportunity to get something free with no strings attached, and uses a direct form of address, arguing with the consumer and inviting him or her to explain the motives behind such a refusal. Here the argument is clear: Everyone likes to get something for nothing. We're offering something for nothing. Everyone ought to be glad to accept what we're offering. Its effect as argument might be demonstrated if sufficient numbers of consumers out of the number who read the post-script out of the number who opened the envelope in the first place respond because they can't think of a reason not to respond.

While it may be possible to spell out some general principles for the presentation of the "argument" of the direct mail letter, the individual letters will always vary according to the nature of the product, the character of the audience, and the persona the advertiser wants to project. To see these rhetorical elements in action we need to turn our attention to some specific artifacts.

A direct mail advertisement from *Business Week* begins with a brief preamble to the letter:

> It's no simple task to develop a dazzling
> talent for business (the silver tongue,
> the golden touch, the mind like a steel trap).
>
> But now the first step, at least, can be easy
> and free of risk . . .
>
> A trial month of Business Week *free!*

The preamble introduces the central idea of the letter to follow and some of the themes the letter will elaborate on at greater length.

The letter itself begins:

I'm sure it's happened to you at a business meeting . . . or during a gathering of friends.

Someone makes a rash comment about the state of the art in your industry. You have hard knowledge on the subject—and make a point that sets things straight.

There are nods of agreement around the room. People appreciate your insights and the way you expressed them.

You have made your presence felt . . .

From this point on, the writer, identified as the publisher of *Business Week*, makes the pitch concerning the magazine by opening with "I'd like to suggest how this experience could become a *regular* occurrence (not just an occasional pleasure)," offering a free month's subscription to the magazine, and giving examples of the contents. At various points in the letter he returns to themes announced in the preamble: "After a whole month of this, I think you'll notice a difference in your business discussions with colleagues. You'll be well on your way to that *silver-tongued readiness of expression* that's so critical in leading other people"; "Each week you'll read about heroes or heroines of industry whose talent or success will inspire you to perfect *your own golden touch*"; "Don't be surprised if your mind grows so sharp and eager that it *closes like a steel trap* around every new business opportunity" [their emphases].

The anecdotal opening of the letter serves a number of purposes: it engages the reader's curiosity by ostensibly talking about him; it identifies the persona of the advertiser as being plain, direct, and supportive; it makes the reader identify with the "you" in the letter. The references to "you" and "I" personalize the letter and give intimacy to the relationship between speaker and listener, and occasional contractions ("you'll," "I'd," "it's") give the language a more conversational tone than formal full spellings.

The same passage also helps establish the identity of the targeted consumer. It has to be someone who can identify with the situation in the anecdote, either because it's happened to him or because it hasn't but he wishes it would. He is someone who sees himself as intelligent, personable, hard working, responsible, and probably not as far up the ladder of success as he feels he deserves to be, someone who can be encouraged by the possibility of regularly "making his presence felt." The emphasis in the letter on the publication helping the reader to be more successful implies that the reader isn't completely successful already.

Much of the central and largest portion of the letter identifies the kinds of news stories, profiles, and features that *Business Week* regularly publishes, but the transitions between them are usually couched in terms of service to the reader, implying that all this information is somehow expressly useful to the individual businessman. The attention to the reader's success, the identification of the reader with the success story that opens the letter, and the flattery of the salutation ("Dear Executive") and the postscript ("We make *Business Week* available only to middle and upper management executives. This . . . is a personal invitation to *you*.") all appeal to the reader's sense of self and reinforce the image of the advertiser as sincere, helpful, and supportive.

In addition to the ethical and pathetic appeals just mentioned, the letter has a logical appeal as well, essentially arguing that reading *Business Week* will make the reader more successful both personally and professionally. But the argument is made cautiously, never explicitly claiming to guarantee success but always implying it, as when the reader is told, "I think you'll notice a difference in your business discussions with colleagues" or "Don't be surprised if you develop a sixth sense . . . [or] if your mind grows . . . sharp and eager" or "See how much it can add to your decision-making powers. Your executive charisma. Your personal security."

In other words the appeal to reason in this letter is based upon an incomplete syllogism:

Possessing information brings success.

*Business Week* provides information.

(*Business Week* provides success.)


Advertising is often built upon an implied syllogism which can seldom be stated overtly because it is seldom true or valid; claims are usually exaggerated, which is what makes advertising deceptive. Even if we accept the major and minor premises above, that possessing information brings success and that *Business Week* provides information, it is still unable to support the implied conclusion and therefore unwilling to claim it, and at the same time it is reluctant to admit that reading the magazine may have no connection with the reader's success or failure.

A key example of the fuzziness of the logical appeal in this letter is the sentence: "Each week you'll read about heroes and heroines of industry whose talent for success will inspire you to perfect *your own golden touch.*" It is followed by three examples of dynamic people in business, which is chiefly what the sentence is intended to introduce. But the underlined words, echoing back to the preamble to the letter, throw the emphasis onto the *reader's* potential accomplishments and away from the words "inspire you to perfect" which place the responsibility for success on the reader.

In this direct mail example from *Business Week* the persuasion is built upon a sense of the audience's needs and an implicit claim to be able to satisfy them, a rather common approach to the pitch. In another example the emphasis is on the reader's sense of identity.

One direct mail solicitation from *The Atlantic Monthly* is a four-page letter emphasizing the history of the magazine and selling subscriptions through promotion of both the magazine itself and an anthology of selections published over the magazine's 125-year history. The implied syllogism runs something like this:

> *The Atlantic Monthly* has a tradition of excellence.
>
> In the past its writers were the very best.
>
> Thus today its writers are the very best.

The syllogism is hardly valid, but the appeal is on several levels. The most overt is the chance to get something for free along with the regular subscription; the anthology is only available with a subscription to the magazine. If you want the book you have to have the magazine; if you were considering the magazine, the bonus gift may help you decide upon it. Magazine subscriptions routinely work that way, but that means of persuasion is economic, not rhetorical.

The first three paragraphs set the tone for the rhetorical development of the letter:

It began at a dinner party in May 1857.

Among the guests—Ralph Waldo Emerson, Henry Wadsworth Longfellow, and Oliver Wendell Holmes. The conversation—Americans needed a publication where the finest contemporary writers and thinkers could express their views. The result—a new magazine that helped change the shape of literature, art and politics for the next 125 years—*The Atlantic*.

Nathaniel Hawthorne. Mark Twain. Jack London. John Galsworthy. Gertrude Stein. Ernest Hemingway. Raymond Chandler. John Updike. Robert Coles. This is just a small sampling of those who have contributed to *The Atlantic* in the past 125 years. Throughout its history, no other magazine has attracted such an impressive assemblage of prominent literary figures.

While the letter goes on to discuss current authors and articles, it relies heavily on the "impressiveness" and "prominence" of the literary names it drops throughout. Sometimes the name-dropping is deceptive—at that dinner party Holmes named the magazine and James Russell Lowell, unnamed in the letter, became its first editor. Emerson had little to do with it and doesn't show up in the anthology.

The argument about the greatness of the magazine lies chiefly in the fame of its contributors; no attempt is made to argue the particular merit of the pieces these figures produce. Even later in the letter the promotion of the anthology focuses on content rather than significance:

Mark Twain at his ornery best.

Harriet Beecher Stowe on the "shocking truth" about Lord Byron's wife. Revelations so controversial they cost *The Atlantic* hundreds of subscribers.

Moreover, the letter neglects to mention that the non-fiction pieces have been cut, some rather drastically.

But the strength of the letter's argument is not in its logic but in its ethos. In effect the ethos of the magazine, rather than the persona of the letter, is the focus of attention here. Since it can't argue, as *Business Week* can, that it can *do* something for the reader, it argues that it *is* something the reader ought to respect or admire and be interested in reading, if the reader is a certain kind of person.

The kind of person the reader is urged to be and that the magazine wishes to represent its reader as being (or perhaps becoming if they read the magazine) is spelled out at the top of the third page of the letter:

*Atlantic* readers are unique. They certainly value fresh thinking. They appreciate good style; are as likely to be interested in art as in science, in music as in politics. *Atlantic* readers have always sought the fresh perspective. We suspect you do too.

The appeal is to people who are not *Atlantic* readers who would like to believe that they are the kind of reader the description refers to. This is not necessarily deceptive; the editors may actually see their readers in exactly those terms, see their magazine as providing something for exactly those kinds of readers, and the readers themselves are unlikely to continue the initial subscription for very long, if in fact they begin it at all, if they don't see the magazine as speaking to interests they think they have or ought to have or would like to have. The structure of the argument, divided equally between the past and the present (or more accurately, the distant past and the immediate past), is one that emphasizes the identity of the magazine, its ethos, and it is chiefly the weight of that which will persuade the reader in this example.

Opponents of popular culture and rhetoric alike have often argued that the chief interest of them both is pleasing the audience; as we have already seen, that view is a gross oversimplification of a fact of life—a commercial culture has to be purchased by someone who is persuaded that he ought to buy it; a presentation of evidence or opinion has to be presented to someone and has no force unless that someone is persuaded of its efficacy or validity. Picasso's paintings and Michael Jackson posters move on the marketplace under the same principles; philosophy and propaganda and advertising are all convincing for the same combination of discourse elements. As we have already seen, while the same elements of an advertising communication triangle may always be interacting, the emphasis or weight given to each element will vary with the advertisement.

*Business Week* and *The Atlantic Monthly* both make appeals to their audiences, but *Business Week*'s persuasive power lies chiefly in its logos and *Atlantic*'s chiefly in its ethos. For an example of a persuasive piece chiefly emphasizing an appeal to the audience's sense of identity, we need turn elsewhere, to the approach taken by *Esquire*.

Here the appeal to the audience begins before the formal opening of the letter, in a section placed above the salutation:

Yes, now there *is* a magazine written with *you, your goals,* and *your life-style* in mind . . . *Like you,* it can be *brash* when it needs to be . . . *sophisticated* when it wants to be . . . *charming* when it pays to be . . . and *witty* nearly every chance it gets.

The underlined words make obvious connections: you, your goals, your life-style; like you, brash, sophisticated, charming, witty. The consumer who envisions himself in these terms—or at least wishes he could—is invited to read on and the letter appeals to specific interests and concerns of such readers:

Will your *height* help you make it to the top of the corporate heap? How about your face . . . your marital status . . . or a *fake* college degree?

Now that more *women* are executives and up-and-coming managers, do *you* know the *new rules* for sexual politics in the office?

Tax shelters—everybody's pitching one, everybody swears by one . . . so what are the odds that you'll be swearing *at*, rather than *by*, that "can't miss" proposition?

If you enjoy keeping up with all the changes taking place today in the boardroom . . . the bedroom (and every place in between!) . . . if you relish reading about uncommon men (like yourself?), uncommon women, and uncommon events, ideas, and places to be . . . I think you'll be pleased to learn about an exciting new magazine.

The emphasis on "you" is the primary one of the letter, particularly the sense of the potential reader as hip, modern, and challenged by a rapidly changing society. By the end of the letter the emphasis has changed to the magazine itself ("as brash, sophisticated, charming, and witty as it has to be to get—and keep—your attention") but still in the context of serving the reader. The implication of the final phrase is "to get and keep the attention of someone as brash, sophisticated, charming, and witty as you are, dear reader." The implied syllogism is something like this:

You are a brash, sophisticated, charming, and witty man in need of a magazine that speaks to contemporary concerns.

We are a brash, sophisticated, charming, and witty magazine addressing contemporary concerns.

You need us.

The success of that message depends upon the reader's acceptance of the appeal to his self-image.

The direct mail examples we have been examining in this chapter are all from magazines, but the principles of rhetorical analysis apply no matter what the example. The direct mail solicitation is sent with the purpose of persuading the reader to invest money in or on a specific enterprise, be it the publishers of *The Wall Street Journal* trying to sell subscriptions, Charlton Heston trying to sell memberships in the American Film Institute, Katharine Hepburn trying to solicit contributions to Planned Parenthood, or Ronald Reagan trying to drum up support for the Republican Party. Such a variety of letters on such a variety of topics is nonetheless bound together by that one single purpose and by the conventions of the epistolary mode— these are, after all, letters. The individuality of the specific direct mail letter comes from the character of the writer it creates (although these may often be very similar) and the character of the product created as well, from the kind of reader it suggests it is addressed to and the kind of emotional response it wants to trigger in the reader it does reach, and from the kind of argument it makes, whether implicitly or explicitly, partly or completely.

The ways in which ethos, logos, and pathos operate in direct mail advertising are, upon analysis, rather straightforward and obvious, principally because the mode is one of direct communication. The advertising communication triangle we have identified in this chapter is similarly applicable to all advertising; however, the various modes of advertising don't always use direct address, nor are they as reliant upon verbal communication. The change in media changes the way the rhetoric of advertising is presented; nonetheless, as we shall see in the chapters which follow, the same rhetorical elements are present, and a careful rhetorical analysis of them reveals how they create their effects.

# 4

# The Rhetoric of Print Advertising: The Visual Pitch

It may be said that all advertising falls on a continuum between direct persuasion, in which the rhetorical elements are expressed chiefly through language, and indirect persuasion, in which the rhetorical elements are less overt and expressed chiefly through actions and images. Direct mail advertising is the embodiment of the verbal pitch; at the other end of the continuum is the television commercial. Print advertising, the magazine and newspaper ads which make up the bulk of most publications, falls between these two poles by adding to the verbal elements a rhetorical approach heavily dependent on images. These two approaches usually complement one another in a successful advertisement and together comprise the rhetoric of print advertising.

Visual advertising is fully as rhetorical as direct mail solicitation. It establishes an ethos for the product, the company, or the service; it appeals to the emotions of the consumer; and it "argues" for the purchase of the product or service in a variety of ways, although the argument may be in fact the least important "proof" attended to by the advertiser. Like direct mail, print advertising is targeted at selected audiences. Products are advertised in specific magazines likely to be read by the average consumer of that product; some products are advertised in different ways in different magazines, adjusting to the nature of the audience. A national ad campaign in a major weekly magazine might feature a middle-class, vaguely mid-western white couple; the same product advertised in a black magazine would feature an upwardly mobile black couple; in a men's magazine, a young single. The product doesn't change, but the advertising makes rhetorical shifts directed at specific audiences.

We can see the effect of these demographic factors by looking at specific ads; for example, ads targeted for different age groups appearing in two diverse magazines like *Rolling Stone* and *Newsweek*. The approaches used in such magazines by a company like De Beers vary according to the nature of the audience. In a single campaign, ads will be laid out essentially the same; in the De Beers ads a close-up of one or two people dominates the page. The text supports or reinforces the image and offers the rationale for the purchase. But the sense of the persona of the ad may differ.

In the De Beers series of ads the speaker is always a customer. In one ad, targeted for the older, more affluent, more middle-class readership of *Newsweek*, a man and a woman are embracing with their eyes closed; both have gray streaked hair although the woman is apparently somewhat younger than the man and her age is more indeterminate. The man holds a diamond ring and the woman's hand is touching his, as if he is about to slip it on her finger. In the middle of the picture, in stark white lettering very near the ring, are the words "I still do," an allusion to previous wedding vows. The couple are in effect repledging their nuptials. The caption, with a closer view of the ring, reads: "The Diamond Anniversary Ring. A band of diamonds that says you'd marry her all over again." At the very bottom is the company slogan: "A diamond is forever. De Beers." Small letters just under the picture inform us that "The ring shown is available for about $2,600. Prices may vary."

Obviously the weight of the rhetoric in this ad is in its emotional appeal, the attempt to make the consumer identify with the people in the picture, be touched in some way by the intimacy and affection displayed, and want to replicate it in his own life. The caption is spoken not by the man in the picture who says "I still do" but by the company to a listener who is not only the man but the reader as well: "A band of diamonds that says *you'd* marry her all over again." The implied argument of the scene is that this happy, tender moment was aided by the company—they provide the ring which allows this man to renew his marriage vows in this intimate and touching way, and they are able to do the same for the reader. The attitude of the caption is approving and encouraging—the idea that the advertiser is chiefly in business to serve the public is a constant element of perhaps a majority of advertising.

But this particular De Beers ad, with its emphasis on people who have "made it," who don't flinch at a $2,600 price tag, and have a marriage durable and secure enough to allow an anniversary celebration after a passage of years, is not aimed at the readers of *Rolling Stone*, where the emphasis is on younger people who are less financially secure, more socially active, more hedonistic. An ad in *Rolling Stone* for De Beers shows a close-up of an attractive young woman wearing braids, one strand of which she is chewing coyly with bright white teeth and holding with a hand that sports a diamond ring. She has little make-up, her hair is tousled, and she wears a sweatshirt. Her eyes are bright and merry. The caption above the picture reads: "I couldn't live without her, so I gave her a big incentive to stick around." The theme of this ad is the same as that of the *Newsweek* ad—that a diamond ring symbolizes and makes explicit private feelings. The voice of the "man" goes on underneath the picture: "I wanted to get Beth a diamond engagement ring as big and beautiful as our future together looked. A diamond that told the world that this wonderful woman wasn't marrying just anyone. She was marrying me." The language here, the casual syntax, the simple vocabulary, suggests youth, earnestness, sincerity.

One level of the emotional appeal is to the expression of tender feelings, the expectation that a man in love will feel his beloved deserves some kind of visual proof to others of that love. But a second level of the appeal to the audience is financial. The character goes on: "Now I'd found out that today a good guideline for getting the most beautiful diamond you can afford is to spend about 2 months salary. So 2 months it was. And as proud of her as I am, she's even prouder of that ring." Small print solicits requests for a booklet, "Everything You'd

Love to Know . . . About Diamonds," and a series of photos in the corner of the picture illustrates the varying sizes and price range of diamonds. A significant portion of the ad then is educational—it informs the novice about the nature of diamond buying and promotes the image of De Beers as helpful, open, reliable, the friend to those who want to do something for the person they love. The appeal is specific and direct and geared to the audience it's targeted for rather than a broad general audience.

The argument of both these ads essentially is an enthymeme: Buy a diamond for the one you love because it shows the world you love her. The implied syllogism is: A gift of diamonds shows other people how a woman is regarded by her lover/husband. You want the world to know how you feel about your beloved. Therefore, you ought to buy her a diamond.

In addition to the establishment of identifiable audiences, print ads establish an identifiable ethos. The De Beers' ethos is fairly consistent, constant, and perceptible through the ads they offer. In many advertisements, however, the ethos of the product, company, or service is clearly the principle means of persuasion. For example, ads which trade on identification with celebrities or recognizable personalities attempt to establish an ethos which the consumer is to equate with the advertiser.

In a series of ads, Cutty Sark promoted its Scotch whisky by identification with prominent figures from various walks of life. Each ad has a layout in which the face or bust of the personality fills the upper and center section of the ad, an illustration identifying the figure appears below and to the right of him, a text appears immediately to the right of the figure, and a caption across the top makes a toast. At the bottom of the picture the product is identified by an extremely close detail of the label, a hand holding a glass with two ice cubes, an etching of a clipper ship, and the legend: "The Scotch with a following of leaders. Cutty Sark."

An example typical of this campaign is the Curt Flood ad for Cutty Sark featuring an extreme close-up of a black man looking up and wearing a serious expression. A giant baseball is pictured on a baseball diamond with a rainbow coming out of it, apparently standing for aspiration. The caption reads: "Some people think you can't beat the system. Here's to those who show the way." The text describes Curt Flood's career in baseball and his successful challenge of the trading system in the Supreme Court, and claims "that opened doors for every baseball player in America." Then the text concludes "So today, a lot of people salute Curt Flood. Including those who make his favorite Scotch, Cutty Sark." The ad is ostensibly about the baseball player, not the Scotch, but the implications are clear—the implied enthymeme is either "You should drink Cutty Sark because Curt Flood does" or "You should drink Cutty Sark because people who admire pacesetters of the society make Cutty Sark." Neither of these is a very successful argument as an argument, although it may be successful as an ad.

Another example of a Cutty Sark ad which makes clearer the distance between the ethos and the product is the Charles Dickens ad. Its caption reads: "Here's to those who've taught us the true spirit of Christmas," and it shows Dickens looking dreamily before him while he holds a pen poised above paper and characters from *A Christmas Carol* appear on either side of him. The text extolls the book and concludes: "We at Cutty Sark toast the spirit of Christmas and those who keep it alive. And hope that you, too, will raise a glass to everyone who's shown you what Christmas is about." Obviously the toast should be made with Cutty Sark, but here the identification is with a subject who doesn't or didn't use the product—rather it is with an attitude. The ethos of the product is linked with forerunners, accomplishers, leaders, and seeks identification with those consumers who might like to feel that they are in some way supporting the values these luminaries stand for by buying a particular Scotch. This kind of identification of consumer with product is illogical but often successful—people may buy according to the image they have of themselves or the image they would like to have of themselves more often than they buy for the specific qualities of the product.

To illustrate this point further we need only glance at several other drink advertisements. Ads for Yukon Jack, 100 Proof Imported Liqueur made with Blended Canadian Whiskey, center on the mystique of the trademark figure. In one ad, above a picture of a dark man in black furs standing alone looking at a vista of snow and rugged terrain, a quote from a Robert Service poem identifies the figure as the kind of man who doesn't "fit in," who rejects the bonds of family and friendship to relentlessly roam the world, a restless loner. A slogan just above the picture of the liqueur and its name calls it "the Black Sheep of Canadian liquors" and the text further confuses the identity of the trademark figure and the product with the words: "Yukon Jack is truly a spirit unto itself." The ethos is drawn from an emphasis on individuality and non-conformity and the ad's appeal is directed to people who seek that identification with themselves, whether overtly or vicariously.

Another ad for a liqueur, Southern Comfort, establishes a different ethos. Under a picture of two young couples in sportswear sipping orange juice and liqueur mixed drinks from glasses marked "Southern Comfort," the text reads: "Everyone Needs a Little Comfort. The temperature was hot and the competition hotter. Now's the time to serve up the cool, refreshing taste of Southern Comfort and orange juice. We call this thirst-quenching combination 'O. J. Comfort.' Your guests will call it delicious!" The youthful vitality of the people in the picture, the implication that they are couples, that they entertain other couples, that they drink to quench their thirst, that they are attractive, all create an ethos for the product that is different from that of Yukon Jack. Where one liqueur promotes its individuality, independence, uniqueness (and thus imparts the same qualities to whomever drinks it), the other promotes its universality and physical and social utility—it "quenches thirst" and meets the approval of guests and thus imparts to its user social acceptability and a sense of comfort.

In the advertisements I have been reviewing here I have concentrated particularly on their pathos and ethos, because the goal of much advertising is chiefly identification of the product and recognition—that is, the product is associated with certain attitudes or behaviors or personalities, and beyond that point the advertiser chiefly seeks recognition of the product when the consumer confronts it. That kind of purpose demands the establishment of a relationship between product and consumer rather than a logical motivation for purchasing.

Walker Gibson, in his study of modern American prose styles, *Tough, Sweet and Stuffy*, states the case this way:

In adwriting, tone is everything. The writing problem is to fabricate an assumed reader who has to be an attractive person with whom the real reader may be expected to identify cheerfully. Secondly, he must be an admirer or user, or highly prospective admirer or user, of the writer's product. The assumed reader is specifically defined, with considerable detail. . . .

The frequency of the word *You* in AROMA [Advertising Rhetoric of Madison Avenue] is over twice what it was in Tough Talk. We are directly assaulted. Not only are we addressed personally by the pronoun, but we are frequently commanded in imperative verbs, or forced to respond to rhetorical questions ("Why not try . . . ?"). Meanwhile every linguistic device known to man is brought to bear on the language to secure intimacy with the reader. For example we have a whole punctuation system appropriate to informal, colloquial expression.[1]

Gibson's description helps explain the ways that the ethos and pathos of an ad are created. He calls such a prose style "Sweet Talk," to distinguish it from "Tough Talk," the language of certain kinds of fiction, and "Stuffy Talk," the language of certain kinds of academic prose. His generalized description of the Sweet Talker is an appropriate outline of the ethos of print advertising:

A Sweet Talker is not at all a hard man who has been around. He addresses me directly ("you"), and when he says "You" he doesn't mean just anybody, he means *me*. He is not a passionate or self-centered man, more concerned with his own feelings than with my needs and desires. On the contrary, he goes out of his way to be nice to me. He defines me as a very particular person with identifiable qualities. (This is of course a problem because they may not be qualities I possess or desire.) He may use the rhetorical devices of informal speech (contractions, fragments, eccentric punctuation) to secure his intimacy with me.[2]

To some degree this description of the Sweet Talker and the relationship he attempts to establish with his reader is applicable to the ethos and pathos attempted in most advertising, although Gibson would agree that within the category of Sweet Talker there can be a range of personae.

Gibson's comments also serve to reinforce the sense in which ethos and pathos are more essential to the rhetoric of advertising than logos is. Logos is the least developed element of proof in advertising, but it is nonetheless still present and observable. In classical rhetoric Aristotle and others developed the concept of common topics (*topoi*) as a means of invention, an aid to generating and organizing an argument; the logos of advertising draws upon these kinds of topics, wittingly or unwittingly, in four main ways: definition, comparison, relationship, and testimony.

Definition, in rhetorical terms, is an attempt to set the limit of meaning for a subject, in effect to make clear the ways in which the subject is understood by the person delivering the argument. The classic example is: "Man is a rational animal." From this definition, from this accepted premise, a number of arguments might develop. In advertising the definition may be the entire argument. A recent series of advertisements for Camel cigarettes showed the same model, a rugged, tousled outdoorsman, in various wild or rough settings—for example, sitting on a large tree stump in khaki and boots in the middle of a forest, various equipment in the foreground—with the caption: "Camel. Where a man belongs." This is a simple definition—in effect, "Camels are a cigarette smoked by rugged outdoorsmen"—but, like most advertising, it trades on associations and double meaning. In this case the definition is not a particularly accurate one, but the advertisement probably is less interested in accuracy—there is no logical connection between a brand of cigarettes and a concept of manliness—than in identification of the product with the image in the ad. The definition is deceptive because the caption refers as much to the locale of the picture as to the cigarette, as if we might translate it to mean, "Camel is the cigarette men smoke when they're in the places they belong or would like to be."

A second common topic is comparison, a common means of organizing an argument. In an ad for Taittinger Champagne, for example, the visual image is of an unopened bottle of champagne and a glass with champagne in it. The caption reads:

"Taittinger Champagne. It spoils you for anything else." The implication is a comparison with other champagnes or other wines. Obviously the comparison is weak because unspecified—what are we comparing the product with?—but a good deal of comparison ads are equally vague. In an ad depicting a marching band in vivid colors walking across a mirror—visually reinforcing the idea of accurate reproduction—a caption for a video cassette reads: "Don't just tape it. TDK it." The implication is that TDK video tape is by comparison so much superior to other tape that we need to identify it differently, separately. The copy begins: "TDK video tape mirrors life," offers several non-comparative statements which the caption implies are comparative ("Play after play images stay crisp. Sound is reproduced faithfully"), and makes one comparative statement ("Our video cassettes are made to tolerances 250% higher than industry standards."). It ends by repeating the caption. The comparison is not fully developed or hardly developed at all.

The third kind of topic is relationship, such as cause and effect. For example, in a series of ads pretending to offer advice, RCA Videodiscs offered one showing three delighted children watching an RCA Videodisc player and peppered the copy with covers of discs. The caption read: "Hint #7 from RCA Videodiscs. How to Keep Your Kids Off the Street." The concept behind the ad was that purchase of this product would have a beneficial effect on the children and on the parents' peace of mind. The copy continued the theme of the caption:

Want to keep your kids from trampling the neighbors' geraniums? Like to know they're in the house and out of the mud?

With the magic of the RCA Video Disc System, you'll know your kids are right at home. After all, what child could walk out on *The Muppet Movie*? Or *Charlie Brown*? Or a *Disney Cartoon Parade*? . . .

And wouldn't you rather have them entertained with *Superman* than out entertaining mischief? Or watching *Grease* instead of getting it on their clothes?

We could say a great deal about the implications of this ad— the ethos of the company as childcare dispenser, the pathos of the attention to fear for the child's well-being and social responsibility, the stereotyping of the children and parents and the assumptions about the family unit suggested—but the main emphasis I'd like to make is on the cause/effect relationship of the ad's organization: "If you purchase this system, your children will not get into mischief of any kind."

Finally, the fourth most common topic used in print advertising is testimony, which can take several forms. One is the direct testimonial, a statement of trust or approval by a purchaser or user; in an ad for women's lingerie, an inset photo of a woman identified as Darleen Rubin, photojournalist, is placed above copy reading in part: "It's my choice to wear Trendsetters. Sure, I could spend more, but I'm past that. I love the styling and comfort and I'm smart enough to enjoy the value."

Another form of testimony is the argument from authority, not solely by having a person in a positon of knowledge speak for the product, as when, say, a tennis pro is pictured endorsing a particular brand of racquet or balls, but also by having a celebrity of almost any kind serving as spokesperson. For example, in an ad for Tandy Corporation personal computers sold at Radio Shack outlets, actor Bill Bixby is pictured with a Tandy 1000 PC; the text never mentions him and simply compares the advertiser's product to that of a rival company, but clearly the reader is expected to identify him and to transfer his authority as actor, celebrity, and television star to authority as computer user.

In another example, actor William Shatner is pictured in an empty room bathed in a blue light from presumably the glow of the moon and stars through glass doors with the caption: "Does lowering your thermostat make your inner space feel like outer space?" The ad, for Kero-Sun portable kerosene heaters ("We bring comfort to inner space"), never mentions the actor by name but clearly trades on recognition of his role as Captain Kirk of the Starship Enterprise in the television and movie series *Star Trek*. The presence of Shatner makes the outer space connection in the slogan more tangible and transfers to the product some of the authority of his role. Authority in advertising may be no more than celebrity testimonial, but the bigger the celebrity, the more authority he or she brings to the product by transference rather than by actual authority.

Yet another form of testimony is statistics, the use of numbers to suggest the weight of evidence. In fact, statistics are often a significant argument for some issues, but in advertising they are chiefly used to promote the band-wagon effect, the argument that the consumer should buy something or do something chiefly because so many other consumers have done it. A clear example of this approach is a two-page advertisement for Wang Computers consisting solely of a brief, narrow column of text with the company logo at the bottom and the number $2,000,000,000.00 in large black figures across the bottom of the white pages. The point is, as the text explains, that "Wang is a two-billion dollar company doing 50% of its business in data processing." It attempts to convince the business consumer that Wang's line of computers for business is preferable to others chiefly on the basis of its corporate assets. As the text argues, "Wang. The last word in words also has strength in numbers."

The kinds of argument that make up advertising suggest that logos is not the chief means of persuasion in print advertising, nor is the rational appeal particularly reliable in most cases. Nonetheless, the relationship that print advertising establishes with its readers is chiefly rhetorical and its rhetorical elements extend beyond the use of text into the use of image. In this way, print advertising is subtler, less overt than direct-mail solicitation—it may catch the reader's attention by its graphics and make its appeals more indirectly. Television commercials elaborate upon that visual element, often in unique ways, but by and large they maintain the same kind of rhetorical relationship with their viewers.

# 5

# The Rhetoric of Television
# Commercials: The Video Pitch

In all advertising the communication triangle is composed of the advertiser, the product, and the consumer. In discussing direct mail and print advertising, we have in effect also been following the history of advertising. The direct address precedes the visual address which subsumes into it elements of the direct address. The video medium of advertising is similarly a development in advertising which subsumes into it the elements of direct address and visual address at the same time that it generates its own particular elements: motion, drama, and effects.

Direct address means that the advertiser has to create a persona to address an assumed general audience as if it were a specific individual audience about a particular service or product—the ethos, pathos, and logos may be subtle, but they are always self-evident. Print advertising, while it may feature testimonials and picture authority figures looking directly at the reader, usually uses an indirect address—that is, the communication of the message is often embodied in the visual details and conveyed by juxtaposition, relation, and attitude, rather than by direct statement. Television commercials also use both direct and indirect address, but they add a dynamic dimension to their message by virtue of their technology. The indirect address may be embodied in changes of state or condition in the course of the commercial or the juxtaposition of several actions with one another.

Another way of making these distinctions clearer would be to describe direct mail solicitation as the rhetoric of exhortation, print advertising as the rhetoric of illustration, and television advertising as the rhetoric of dramatization. The chief distinction between television advertising and other forms is its dynamic quality, its ability not merely to tell or to statically illustrate, but to enact—television commercials are not merely advertising tableaux but advertising parables. Far more than print advertising, they take us beyond the boundaries of what we traditionally think of as the rhetorical situation.

Nonetheless the rhetorical situation is present. Though the mode may have changed to video, the purpose—to sell a product—is the same as it is for other forms of advertising, and the commercial still needs to make an ethical appeal, a pathetic appeal, and a rational appeal.

To illustrate these elements, we need to look at a specific commercial. In the early 1970's a commercial for a finance company ran on Iowa stations using a farm setting. It opened with a wide shot of farmland and a man on a tractor, moved to a closer shot of the farmer shutting off the tractor and mopping his brow, cut to the interior of the house as he enters and reacts to something. In the next shot we see the farmer's wife pinning up the wedding dress of their daughter, who smiles at her father. The reaction shot of the father shows him near tears and perhaps a little concerned. Very quickly we move to a scene of an employee of Thorp Finance cheerily welcoming the dressed-up farmer into his office and shots indicating discussion and approval of a loan. The commercial ends with shots of the bride and her new husband leaving the church after their wedding and the happy embrace of father and mother as the couple drives off. While a voice-over explains the ease with which Thorp makes loans available to working people, the main thrust of the commercial lies in the lyrics of its theme: "You work hard for a living and you deserve credit for that. You work hard for a living and Thorp gives you credit for that."

The effectiveness of this commercial lies chiefly in its pathetic appeal—while all three types of appeal are present in every discourse, some may be so muted or underdeveloped as to seem negligible—nonetheless the appeals of ethos and logos are also present. The appeal to the emotions of the audience lies in the circumstances dramatized in the commercial, which is being broadcast to a primarily agricultural state. A high percentage of viewers must identify with the farmer and be sympathetic to the assertion that he works hard for a living. But the appeal is also to anyone who works hard for a living, of which the farmer may be just one example, and doesn't have enough money. Obviously the commercial has to appeal to working-class rather than affluent people who work hard for a living. A second part of the pathetic appeal is to the values of the family and traditional responsibilities. The daughter's wedding is clearly an additional expense most parents would feel obliged to be generous about, and most working-class parents at least would feel the financial pinch of providing. Finally, the commercial appeals to the viewer's sense of relief by seeing the problem resolved by the procurement of a loan. Thus the mini-drama of the commercial creates sympathy for a hard-working, responsible, loving family man who stands for the audience at large and first creates a conflict for him and then resolves it happily.

The ethos of the advertiser is made explicit in the middle of the commercial, embodied by the clean-cut, gracious, friendly Thorp employee who welcomes the farmer into his office and solves his problem for him. It is also implicit in the assertion that the company gives people loans because they work hard for a living and deserve them. The values of the company are the values of the audience—a respect for hard work, a concern for the family (note that the farmer's financial need is prompted by love of his daughter, not desire for something frivolous), a belief in traditional values. To some extent the ethos is muted and less forceful than the pathos, but it is nonetheless subtly present throughout the commercial.

The logos of the commercial rests chiefly in the slogan sung throughout it: "You work hard for a living and you deserve credit for that. You work hard for a living and Thorp gives you credit for that." Expressed as a syllogism, the argument is this:

People who work hard for a living deserve credit. (Major Premise)

You work hard for a living. (Minor Premise)

You deserve credit for working hard. (Conclusion)

In a sense the commercial dramatizes the syllogism by providing an example: A man is shown working hard for a living and receiving credit from Thorp Finance, ostensibly because his willingness to work hard makes him a good risk. By implication the commercial makes this argument to the viewer: If you are someone who is hardworking and responsible and in need of money for a worthwhile expense, you will be lent money by Thorp Finance. In fact the implication is even stronger—that Thorp will be giving you money as a deserved reward for your hard work.

Obviously there are problems with the argument, which may be lost in the attention to pathos. For one thing, the syllogism is invalid because of equivocation in the term "credit." The first use of the word in the jingle denotes the idiomatic meaning— to give someone credit for something is to acknowledge the value of that action or the actor's intentions in doing it, as in, "You have to give them credit for trying, even though they lost." But the second use of the word denotes the economic meaning—to give someone credit is to allow them to borrow money on the promise of later repayment with interest and the acknowledgment of penalties for the failure to repay. Substituting the specific denotations for the equivocated word, the syllogism really says this:

People who work hard for a living deserve acknowledgment.

You work hard for a living.

Thorp will lend you money for working hard.

(Or: Thorp will allow you to borrow money and pay it back with interest because you work hard.)

A syllogism needs to have a major term, a minor term, and a middle term. In the classic example of syllogism:

All men are mortal.

Socrates is a man.

Therefore, Socrates is mortal.

the major term is "mortal" (the predicate term of the conclusion), the minor term is "Socrates" (the subject term of the conclusion), and the middle term is "men" or "man" (the term that appears in both the major and minor premises but not in the conclusion). In the commercial example the middle term is obviously "work hard" (or "hard workers"), the minor term is "you", and the major term ought to be "credit." But one of the rules for a syllogism to be valid is that "No term may be distributed in the conclusion if it was not distributed in the premise."[1] If we replace "credit" with "acknowledgment" in the major premise and "money" in the conclusion, we see that the major term is actually new to the conclusion. The syllogism ought either to conclude that "Thorp acknowledges your hard work" or to state in the major premise that "Hard workers deserve to be lent money." It should either read "You work hard for a living and you deserve acknowledgment. You work hard for a living and Thorp acknowledges that" or "You work hard for a living and you deserve to be lent money for that. You work hard for a living and Thorp lends you money for that."

The elements of ethos, pathos, and logos are present in every television commercial, but the ways these rhetorical elements are used depends upon the kind of delivery the advertiser elects to make. For example, the commercial may be presented as a direct address, someone representing the company or the product speaking to the consumer directly. Lee Iacocca, the president of Chrysler, speaks to the audience in his capacity as president, asserting the superiority of his product, improvements in production and design, reliability of company service. Ricardo Montalban, also for Chrysler, talks about comfort, luxury, power, and aesthetics. Cliff Robertson for AT&T argues for the experience, availability, and efficiency of his corporation over their competitors. In each case the ethos of the speaker makes a strong appeal, but notice that the ethos is different with each man. Iacocca is a businessman who seems to be arguing from a willingness to put his own personal integrity on the line about his product; Montalban, a celebrity whose persona argues sophistication and experience with luxury; Robertson, an actor who projects authority and sincerity. The commercials draw upon appeals from authority or testimonials, though each is geared to its specific personality.

If the use of an authority parallels the direct address of direct mail solicitation, the illustrative commercial parallels print advertising. In such a commercial the visual image is used for display purposes, much the way a picture is used in print advertising. An example might be the commercial for GE Soft White Lightbulbs, in which a painter works on a portrait of a woman and a child as they sit in the adjusted light of a lamp and the music of Pachebel's "Kanon in D" sounds behind an announcer's voice extolling the virtues of the product. Similarly, car commercials show the automobile in motion or display it statically by itself to show off its design. A third example might be a Purina Cat Chow commercial depicting a series of young cats being fondled and admired by a variety of supposed owners. In such cases the pictures are chiefly illustrative, not attempts to dramatize the uses or values of the products.

A third form of commercial is the dramatization, in which the whole of the commercial is given over to one specific incident in which people respond to one another involving the product. An example would be the A-1 Steak Sauce commercial where the uncle is caught by his nephew putting steak sauce on his hamburger and then proceeds to convince the rest of the family, presumably including the aunt and the nephew's parents, that hamburger is steak and therefore appropriate for steak sauce. By the end of the commercial the two women and the nephew have offered further testimony to the propriety of this behavior; the boy's father remains mute, but cheerful.

Another example would be the series of commercials for Bounty Paper Towels in which Nancy Walker, as Rosie, explains the utility of "new" Bounty and its advantages over other brands or, usually, "old" Bounty, by cleaning up a spill made by a clumsy customer. Though there may be personalities in the commercial, the dramatization concentrates on exemplifying the alleged assets of the product, often with comparisons with competitors or before and after comparisons.

A fourth form of the commercial, similar to the dramatization, is the vignette, which is really a series of dramatizations in a single commercial. The classic description of the vignette commercial is given in Michael Arlen's book *Thirty Seconds* by a film editor working on a commercial for AT&T:

Nowadays, the basic new technique is your vignette commercial. In my opinion it's a classic film approach—meaning that there's often no dialogue, and the style emphasis is on visual, but not gimmicky visual. The key thing to remember about the vignette commercials is that you can get so much information into them. In fact, the vignettes more or less originated in response to the switch from the sixty-second spots to thirty-second spots. They're a wonderful way to pack in information: all those scenes and emotions—cut, cut, cut. Also, they permit you a very freestyle approach—meaning that as long as you stay true to your basic vignette theme you can usually just drop one and shove in another.[2]

The commercial that best illustrates this approach is the one Arlen's book describes, the "Tap Dancing" spot for AT&T's "Reach Out and Touch Someone" campaign. Here in the course of thirty seconds the viewer is exposed to both ends of five separate telephone conversations, one between an old man in a music hall and a little girl wearing tap shoes, another between an Army recruit with a freshly shaven head and a small town barber, a third between two women standing on their heads, a fourth between a rodeo cowboy and a female jockey, and a fifth between a hockey player in the locker room after a game and a small boy in the same uniform in a house.[3] Each vignette is an attempt to illustrate how people with something in common are able to keep in touch with one another although they are far apart, by telephoning.[4]

These four types are not necessarily an exhaustive list of the varieties of television commercials, but they do illustrate the range available, and the ways in which the video medium alters the conventions of the direct mail and print media and, in the dramatization and the vignette, creates conventions unique to itself.

The rhetorical elements in video advertising are used in different ways, with different emphases, depending on the product, the program, the time of day the commercial is to air, the kind of audience it intends to reach. McDonald's Restaurants, for example, have been particularly adept at gearing their commercials for specific markets, running a series of commercials about a clown and a collection of fantasy characters during children's programming, and offering commercials with specifically identifiable figures and background music to reach Southerners, Midwesterners, urban blacks, adolescents, working women, families, and so on. The attempt to limit and target a specific audience is a significant part of many of the more expensive campaigns. For the rest the advertiser has to hope to produce as universal a commercial as possible.

Nonetheless, in all that variety there are predictable ways in which television commercials use rhetorical elements; though each commercial will contain ethos, pathos, and logos, the emphasis will usually be on one over the other and usually in limited ways.

The appeal to reason in television advertising usually takes the form of exhortation (an announcer urging the consumer to buy something or do something; a direct address from a celebrity or authority figure), example (a dramatization, a series of vignettes, or the direct address of a "typical user"), and identification (the establishment of the product identity in the viewer's mind without much attempt to overtly persuade the viewer to use it). All three approaches are common.

The appeal to pathos in television advertising is likely to be stronger than the appeal to logos. Often the appeal to the viewer's sense of family or love of children is a way to make the viewer identify the product in connection with some social good he believes in or, in the case of commercials in which guilt and fear are created, as something that shares his or her opposition to an ill or that is capable of preventing or relieving that ill. For example, in a dramatization for McDonald's, a black working mother is shown busy at the job while her children stare glumly out the window at home. The jingle sympathizes with the need to earn a living and both endorses the desire to be at home with the children and exacerbates the guilt over not being at home. In the end the mother meets the children at McDonald's for supper. McDonald's thus identifies itself with family unity at the same time that it fosters guilt over separation and offers itself as a means to expiate that guilt.

Pathos on television usually accompanies an attempt at identifying the product as the means of alleviating guilt or achieving the romantic or familial goal. McDonald's has also done a commercial extolling the joys of childhood, picturing a series of children in cute, adorable, and typical behaviors, usually in connection with a playground at a McDonald's franchise or while eating identifiably fast-food meals. The song sung throughout is another set of lyrics to the familiar McDonald's jingle, and ends with the lines: "Hey, little lady, hey, little man, try to stay a kid just as long as you can. It's a good time for the great taste of McDonald's." Both the visuals and the ending of the song attempt to promote the idea that eating at McDonald's is an essential part of childhood, and to reinforce that association in both children, who will then ask to eat at McDonald's, and parents, who will associate McDonald's with a place to take the children.

Pathos is seldom utilized on television without some appeal to guilt or fear. As a phone company spokesperson is quoted as saying:

I suppose there's a small element of guilt in some of our advertising, but we try to keep it pretty light. In fact, we prefer to think of it in terms of obligation. . . . You can suggest in an artistic manner that a person might feel better for making a phone call to a faraway friend, but it wouldn't be right to suggest that something terrible will happen to the person if they don't make the call—that they'll lose the girl or the boy and ruin their lives. So what we try to do is keep the obligation level very light and, of course, artistic, and relate it to an upbeat positive theme.[5]

Guilt usually is created by a sense of neglect, of having failed to provide some pleasure for others, be it a phone call or a meal in a fast-food franchise or a specific product. Even Atari's commercials for personal computers have made it seem as if any parent who doesn't buy one for his child is irresponsible and negligent about the child's education and employment prospects. Fear usually is generated as fear of failure, embarrassment, or disapproval, of doing the stupid thing, the wrong thing, the unacceptable thing. American Express pictures couples off on a foreign vacation suddenly confronted by the loss of travelers' checks and in need of help to get them out of the country. Wisk commercials show a man in the act of doing something sociable or helpful being humiliated by "ring around the collar." Other commercials show women being shunned for having dandruff or being admired for wearing the right kind of hosiery. The appeal to a desire for approval and admiration is the converse of the appeal to guilt and fear—it promises what the other threatens, and the threat is implied in the promise.

If the appeal to the emotions of the audience is stronger on television than the appeal to reason, the ethical appeal may be the strongest of all, because it is the rhetorical element that most clearly distinguishes one company from another. For example, the chief difference between advertising for Lowenbrau and Miller High Life Beer lies in the sense of the beer's role in the consumer's life. The slogan for one beer, "Welcome to Miller Time," endorses the view that hard-workng or hard-playing men deserve a reward at the end of their efforts and that Miller is the beer that rewards and relaxes them. The commercial displays high spirits, camaraderie, and sociability. Lowenbrau, on the other hand, endorses the view that the choice of a beer reveals a person's feelings about friends or guests. When the consumer wants to make an occasion special or demonstrate his feelings toward others, the commercial recommends, "Let it be Lowenbrau." Embodied in each establishment of ethos is also a pathetic appeal.

Ethos is important simply because the nature and purpose of so many products are so similar. Beer, it may be argued, is simply beer, detergents are merely detergents, toilet paper only toilet paper. What distinguishes them is the sense of themselves that they create. Commercials for All depict a father and son coming into the house begrimed after working on the car and the mother immediately taking their sweatshirts and washing them. This seems to suggest that the mother's role is distinct from the father's—the father is active and mechanically responsible, the mother is passive and responsible for laundry—but equally important and capable of winning family approval through the use of the advertiser's product. The emphasis seems to be on All as a significant part of the life of a happy family. Wisk, on the other hand, by emphasizing "ring around the collar," promotes itself as a product insuring social approval. In this series of commercials a son is taught by his mother, a young man by his attractive neighbor, a husband by his wife, how to remove embarassing collar stains. The implication is that collar stains negate a man's accomplishments—the son is showing his mother his new apartment, the husband is detailing a special gourmet meal he has prepared for his working wife—and that the advice of a knowledgable woman can correct the situation. There are severe limits to the kinds of claims one can make about detergents and the major manufacturers of any given product usually have a range of alternatives that compete with each other as well as other manufacturer's products, each directed at specific markets or specific claims. Ethos is the chief means to tell them apart.

The commercial can be a unique form of advertising—its medium is far more dynamic and flexible than print advertising and direct mail—and at times it seems to be chiefly dramatic or cinematic rather than promotional. Yet all of its dramatic elements—the creation of character, the generation of conflict and its resolution—and all of its cinematic elements—the movement of the camera, the editing of the film—serve only one purpose, the selling of a specific product or service. That purpose is persuasive, and the means to affect that purpose are rhetorical, though often less overtly so than other forms of advertising. Eventually, when we turn our attention to forms of popular entertainment, we will see that drama and fiction themselves have rhetorical dimensions and draw upon the same rhetorical elements to affect an audience and deliver a message, even when the purpose of the entertainment is not chiefly persuasive. Moreover, when we turn our attention to forms of advocacy we will see the same elements at work, whether implicitly or explicitly. Television commercials are unique because they embody both the rhetoric of advocacy and the rhetoric of entertainment in the service of the rhetoric of advertising.

# Part III

# RHETORIC AND ADVOCACY

# 6

# The Rhetoric of Reviewing:
# Advocacy, Art, and Judgment

Reviewing is a rhetorical act. Whether its subject is a book, a film, a television program, a recording, a concert, a play, an art exhibit, or a dance performance, the critical review always involves a recommendation, whether implicit or explicit, and an attempt to convince readers of the reliability of that recommendation. Its persuasive elements are the standard elements of rhetoric: ethos, logos, and pathos. Every critical review contains these elements not only because they are part of every act of communication but also because they are crucial to establishing the reliability of the reviewer. On some level every critic is an advocate of certain ways of viewing art and forming judgments about it; his success lies in convincing readers that his judgment is sound and that his way of responding to art is valid. He achieves this by advocating his position both on particular works and, either implicitly or explicitly, on the art form in general in a way that persuades his readers to share that position. To be persuasive, the reviewer must attend to the rhetorical elements and, to be analytical about the review, the reader must attend to them as well.

As in every rhetorical situation, the author's purpose significantly influences the handling of rhetorical elements, but the critical review, while extremely flexible as to length and format, is rather constrained as to essential content. Whether directly or indirectly, the author has to describe the work under discussion to let the reader know some fundamental ingredients and to build a context for evaluation. The author also has to evaluate the work and, if he is to be successful, substantiate his evaluation with examples and illustrations from the work. Finally, the author has to make a recommendation, either by expressly stating his opinion or by implying his opinion through his evaluation. Description, substantiation, evaluation, and recommendation are essential content elements in any good review, although they may be presented in any number of explicit and implicit, individual and conglomerate ways. Neal Gabler, at one time film critic for both *Monthly Detroit* and the PBS film review program, *Sneak Previews*, has summed up the reviewer's role that he and his co-host Jeffrey Lyons played in this way: "Jeffrey and I never pretend that we are doing anything more than answering the two questions to which our viewers want answers: What's it about? Is it any good?"[1] At the very least, a competent review should provide the answers to these questions.

But reviews can also go beyond these basic elements to add the element of interpretation. Most critics make a distinction between reviewing and criticism, seeing criticism as an approach to a work that allows for a more intense, more personal, more analytical response. Neal Gabler stressed this aspect of his writing for *Monthly Detroit*, saying, "Criticism for me is a way of giving something back to the movie."[2] In this regard the critical review can be taken beyond the reporting and recommending of reviewing, the function as a consumer's guide, to create a work tied more intimately to the critic's own intellectual experience. David Denby, film critic for *New York Magazine*, selects topics where he has "an edge on the movie," determining what he wants to write by the intensity of his feeling about the work.[3] Criticism thus is more analytical, more involved, more expansive than reviewing and links itself more closely to the critic's understanding of the art form or to his understanding of the world that art represents and also relates to.

Whether it goes deeply into analysis and interpretation or simply describes, evaluates, and recommends, the purpose of the critical review is essentially the same, and it is the treatment of the review's rhetorical elements which determines how successfully it will achieve its purpose and how convincing it will be to its readers.

The author's sense of his audience is one of those rhetorical elements, and it helps determine the handling of the information and the presentation of the author's persona. The audience is sometimes determined by the publication itself—a book review for *Time* would be directed toward a reasonably well-educated general readership, while a review of the same book for *The English Journal* would need to speak to its readers as professional educators who assume the review will connect to their teaching or their professional lives.

The critic's sense of audience shapes the direction of his review from the outset. For example, Tom Mulhern's brief review of Pink Floyd's album *The Wall* in *Guitar Player* is clearly designed for readers who have a special interest:

From the first menacing entrance of David Gilmour's distortion-laden Strat, you know this is Pink Floyd, all right. The multi-tracked and echo-enhanced cleartone guitars on "Another Brick in the Wall" float in and out of earshot while Roger Waters lays down a bass ostinato that sounds as if it were transplanted from an old Motown tune. There is a continuous metamorphosis of moods throughout, yet there is cohesion in the all-pervasive plot. Gilmour's longest and most expressive solo is a 32 bar excursion in "Another Brick in the Wall Part 2," although his licks on the frightening "One of My Turns" are also heavyweights (and perhaps more endearing to Floyd fans). It's not all bombs bursting in air on this double album; a few nice acoustic ditties are also added for good measure.[4]

The emphasis throughout the review is upon the guitar work, and the terminology is specifically directed at an audience which shares the same professional language.

In contrast this unsigned review of the same album in *Billboard* is obviously written for a different kind of reader, the record retailers who consult the magazine for information on new recordings they might stock.

The first Pink Floyd album since 1977's "Animals" is a double-pocket concept album with the title apparently symbolic of the separation between performer and audience. There are other analogies that can be made as to the wall's meaning, yet one thing remains constant and that is Floyd's ability to produce interesting music. There's a lot of music here, most songs short and running the gamut from mainstream textured rock tunes to rather esoteric tracks with voice-overs, electronics, and orchestral backing. For the first time, Floyd has used a major name producer in Ezrin, who has previously worked with Alice Cooper and Kiss. As usual, Roger Waters' lyrics are a standout and the playing is tight. Look for a tour next year.[5]

The review here is more descriptive, more general, and more sales oriented than the previous review.

Each of these two reviews is appropriate for the magazine in which it appears and inappropriate for the other magazine. Distributors need to know more about the album than the quality of its guitar work; guitarists do not need to know about the album's potential for sales. The nature of the publication in which the review appears has much to do with the rhetorical stance of the review itself, even if the difference in audience is not as sharp as in these two examples: film critic Pauline Kael's writing for *The New Yorker* would be no more acceptable to the readers of *Ladies Home Journal* than *LHJ* reviewer Liz Smith's writing would be for readers of *The New Yorker*. These examples suggest the interrelatedness of the author's sense of audience and the audience's sense of the author.

Another rhetorical element is the author's presentation of a persona. Critics like to say that they write for themselves and to some degree they do, particularly when they are most deeply exploring the aspects of a work to which they strongly respond, but they also write with an audience in mind—someone to whom they are trying to make ideas clear and whom they are trying to make laugh, think, or decide. The audience may well be one which thinks like the critic—Pauline Kael would no doubt prefer the readers of *The New Yorker* to the readers of *Ms.* because her compatibility with *New Yorker* readers allows her the freedom to be herself—but the critic nonetheless must present herself with a distinct, if sometimes circumspect, persona.

In some cases the critic's personality is the dominant element in his criticism, as it is with Gene Shalit, Rex Reed, and John

Simon. For a particularly pronounced example, read Joe Fernbacher's review of *The Wall* for *Creem*, which says in part:

*The Wall* is Krell music supreme, a tangled expression of the sheer
nastiness of the 70's, a four sided operetta of the morbid swirling around
a vortex of contradiction and confusion. As a conceptual piece, it's
solid. As a musical entity, its power lies in its awesome ability to un-
derscore the cool imprecisions of chaos confirmed. As an expression
of neurotic beauty, it can hypnotize with gruesome insistence. And as
structured noise, it can turn your nerve endings into concrete road-
ways of carcinomatous joy and short-sheet your sensibilities. In short
this work is a perfect anti-rhythmic parable of neurosis personified
. . . an erosive stroll into the athoid plains of Roger Waters' inner
psychic mechanizations and the rest of the band's overwhelming
amoebaen response to said ideations. Wuzza. Wuzza.[6]

Fernbacher's persona is deliberately flashy, outrageous, energetic, and vague.

In contrast, the persona of Kurt Loder, the critic reviewing
*The Wall* for *Rolling Stone*, is more thoughtful and serious, and
his reference points make him sound knowledgable and delib-
erate:

Roger Waters, who wrote all the words and a majority of the music
here, projects a dark, multi-layered vision of post-World War II Western (and especially British) society so unremittingly dismal and acid-
ulous that it makes contemporary gloom-mongers such as Randy
Newman or, say, Nico, seem like Peter Pan and Tinker Bell. *The Wall*
is a stunning synthesis of Waters' by now familiar thematic obses-
sions.[7]

The reader's confidence in the critic's knowledge, logic, or shared
sensibilities is created by a sense of the persona the critic creates. By delighting, charming, assuring, or intimidating the
reader, the critic may also influence him.

The final element to which an audience or reader reacts is
the critic's treatment of the subject, both in the argument the
critic makes for the position he asserts about the work and also
in the relationship the critic makes between the work under
discussion and an explicit or implicit set of standards, ideas,
and preconceptions about the elements of the work, the genre

of the work, and/or an ideal concept of what such a work ought to be. For example, David Denby doesn't review horror films for *New York* in part because they are not the kind of film his upscale readers are interested in seeing and in part because, as he says, he brings nothing to the viewing of them.[8]

The larger ruling aesthetic into which an individual work is placed affects the response of the critic. On one level this may be mere personal idiosyncrasy, for example, John Simon's contempt for Liza Minelli and Barbra Streisand and adoration for Natassia Kinski, chiefly on grounds of their personal appearance. On another level, this may be a central theoretical or philosophical position, such as Arthur Schlesinger takes in a review of *Blue Collar* which appeared in *Saturday Review*:

The other grievous fault is that the film's target is the United Auto Workers—the union of all unions that has striven most carefully and energetically to prevent precisely the kind of labor racketeering the movie indicts. The union in the movie is called the AAW—presumably the Associated Auto Workers—but the photographs of Walter Reuther hanging on the wall in the office of the crooked union boss leave no doubt about the union the Schraders had in mind.[9]

Schlesinger's assessment of the film is colored by his position on unions in general and on one labor union in particular. For the public and the critics alike, film can often be a kind of Rohrschach test of political or sociological or aesthetic attitudes. Such attitudes are often implicit in reviews and not spelled out, but they color the ways reviewers marshall the concrete evidence they offer, because whether clearly expressed or merely hinted at, whether obvious to the reader or unclear even to the critic, such attitudes determine the judgments critics make about the concrete details of a work.

But it is in the details of the film's description, the point of view the critic establishes at the start of the review, and the evidence he brings in support of that point of view that the argument of the review is made. Often this is the most difficult aspect of the review because, unlike student themes, critics seldom choose a thesis-and-support approach and prefer to blend opinion with detailed description.

To see the rhetorical elements at work we need to examine a single review, one which is typical of the critical review but not an exemplary model of the form. Richard Schickel's review of *Blue Collar* in *Time* may be considered representative:

*Blue Collar* looks as if it might actually have been made by people who wear blue collars when they go to work, instead of turtlenecks, beads, and suede jackets. That is to say, the picture is often awkward as it attempts to slice open the lives of some automobile-assembly-line workers and expose the futility of their existence. In the end, however, *Blue Collar's* lack of slickness, the sense it frequently conveys of being an authentic cry from the heart, gives it a certain distinction.

Sociologists and their journalistic popularizers have been having at the factory hands for some time now. Everyone knows by now that they suffer intense feelings of on-the-job anomie and alienation that show themselves in absenteeism, alcoholism, and other unpleasantries. We have heard that they feel simultaneously exploited (by both their employers and their unions) and ignored (by the rest of society). But such matters are not much discussed in movies. Paul Schrader, previously best known as the writer of *Taxi Driver*, which dealt with another sort of disenfranchisement, deserves high marks for originality as prime mover, director, and co-writer of this new project.

He seems to have trouble with comedy. Early attempts to wring bitter laughter out of the assembly-line conditions and the financial woes of the three central characters (Richard Pryor, Harvey Keitel, and Yaphet Kotto) do not entirely pay off. Still, these scenes help motivate the film's central incident, a robbery of their own union's safe in which the three turn up not the cash they wanted but a ledger hinting at various forms of veniality and corruption. Their attempts to capitalize on the information are ambiguous: they would like to blackmail some money out of the union local, but knowing their leaders are corrupt also stirs reformist impulses in them, and it is their contrary feelings that provide the film's human interest and dramatic suspense. Finally there is hell to pay. Kotto, playing a sometime small-time criminal, is murdered in a particularly grueling way. The union buys off Pryor with a shop steward's job. Keitel finally turns FBI stoolie. In short, their venture into crime and/or conscience, as one could predict from their earlier lives, ends with our heroes getting, as they would surely put it, screwed again. Indeed, at the film's close the two survivors have lost the one good thing in their lives—their sustaining camaraderie.

As a director, Schrader is lucky to have three strong men for his leading roles. Kotto, in particular, gives depth and an odd, worldly-wise dignity to his role as a man who is not as smart as he thinks he is, though in some ways is much wiser than he admits even to himself. None of them, though, gets as much help from Schrader as they could use. He has trouble finding the heart of a scene, trouble keeping the overall tone and tension of his film consistent. There is a power in this story he simply does not realize. Even so, the film shows an honest impulse to open up new realms to the viewer, and there is nothing patronizing, no sense of sociopsychological slumming about it. *Blue Collar* may linger in the mind when a lot of slicker, more easily assimilated movies have passed beyond recall.[10]

The review opens with a paragraph which establishes Schickel's attitude toward the film, that it is awkward but seemingly authentic and distinctive. His second paragraph generally reviews the observations of sociologists and journalists about the difficulties of factory workers and congratulates the film's director, Paul Schrader, for tackling the subject in a movie. Schickel's third paragraph details the plot of the film and draws a conclusion about its ending, that "at the film's close the two survivors have lost the one good thing in their lives—their sustaining camaraderie," tying the plot to the movie's theme. In his fourth and final paragraph, Schickel singles out the performances for praise and says more about Schrader's "trouble finding the heart of a scene" and "keeping the overall tone and tension of his film consistent"; his conclusion that, because of its honesty and sympathy with its subject, it may "linger in the mind when a lot of slicker, more easily assimilated movies have passed beyond recall," implies a recommendation of the film despite its flaws.

Much in the review is implied rather than stated. For example, when Schickel writes, *"Blue Collar* looks as if it might actually have been made by people who wear blue collars when they go to work, instead of turtlenecks, beads, and suede jackets," he is making reference to a body of people other than his readers. His implied sense of his audience as better educated and more affluent than the characters in the film runs through the review ("We have heard that they feel . . . ," "the film shows an honest impulse to open up new realms of experience to the viewer"). Schickel also implies his own values: when he says, "such matters are not much discussed in movies," and that therefore Schrader "deserves high marks for originality," he suggests that such matters *ought* to be discussed in movies. He also gives a sense of what he values in opting to endorse the film in spite of its technical flaws and because of its subject and its sense "of being an authentic cry from the heart."

Such statements not only tie Schickel to a broader view of film and its role in society, they also help to give a sense of his ethos, as a caring, sympathetic, even sensitive individual. At the same time his remarks about the techniques suggest a knowledgeable, alert observer who understands the craft of filmmaking. In some sentences he is able to convey both sides of his persona at once: "the picture is often awkward as it attempts to slice open the lives of some automobile-assembly-line workers and expose the futility of their existence." Finally, Schickel is trying to endorse the film because of its sense of the working man's life, and his evidence continually emphasizes that sense and how the film transmits it, so that the details about blue collar workers together with the support of Schickel's acceptance of those details as accurate argue strongly for his position about the film.

As a rhetorical act, criticism attempts to persuade the reader of the validity of the reviewer's opinion; it advocates a specific position on art or ideas. The measure of a good critic may be both flexibility and consistency, that is, the ability to avoid a narrow, dogmatic position at the same time that he establishes a clear, continually applied set of values. The flexibility is important because art is so various, and the temptation to judge from individual taste can lead a reviewer to condemn all but a narrow range of artifacts. Consistency is important because it establishes the reliability of the reviewer. The reader is better able to accept an opinion with which he disagrees from someone whose position is grounded in some clear, reasonable aesthetic than an opinion grounded in whimsy which contradicts an earlier position. The first establishes a reliable ethos, the second undermines each argument by the reader's perception of an unreliable persona. The professional reviewer thus establishes not only an ethos for the individual review but an ethos for his criticism as a whole, and the reader's familiarity with the reviewer's work will contribute to his response to an individual review.

Unlike advertising, which in effect "advocates" certain positions concerning products and services, advocacy always endorses implicit or explicit positions about ideas, issues, or interpretations. Advertising's purpose is commercial; advocacy is more intellectual, if not always necessarily intelligent. Advocacy is closer to what we traditionally regard as the province of rhetoric, a concern for probable truth and an effort to convince others of the validity of one's own position. As such it is more subject to a rhetorical analysis that focuses on the strength of its argument, its logos. More than advertising, which can concentrate chiefly on impact, advocacy demands a more sustained presentation whose appeals are grounded in a specific context, supported by evidence, and produced by careful analysis and interpretation. In reviewing, advocacy is drawn from an underlying aesthetic (whether consistent and fully developed or not), and the evaluations made of specific artifacts reveal the critic's sense of both what certain kinds of art *ought* to be like and also the degree to which the particular work under discussion has measured up to those standards. Thus both as discourse and as advocacy, reviewing is a rhetorical act.

# 7

# The Rhetoric of Speculation: Science and Pseudoscience, Advocacy and Evidence

In his influential and important book, *A Theory of Discourse*, James L. Kinneavy divides discourse into four aims, each of which emphasizes a separate section of the communication triangle. *Expressive* discourse focuses on the encoder, the speaker or writer of the discourse; *literary* discourse, on the signal itself, the speech or the text; *persuasive* discourse, on the decoder, the listener or reader; and *referential* discourse, on the reality that the discourse discusses.[1] Kinneavy includes a "crucial caution" about overlap, warning that despite his systematic separation of the aims of discourse, it should never be presumed that each aim functions in complete isolation from the others; for example, "persuasion as a matter of course incorporates information about the product, maybe even some valid scientific proof of its superiority. . . . Scientific proof includes persuasive aspects."[2]

The essential difficulty in any taxonomy is the misleading exclusiveness of its categories. In Kinneavy's system of discourse, the aims are defined chiefly in terms of their emphases and every kind of discourse, no matter what its focus, nonetheless has rhetorical elements—especially the interaction of writer, reader, and reality. To analyze an example of referential discourse with attention solely to its presentation of reality, overlooks the essential dynamics of every discourse situation.

That caution taken, we can utilize Kinneavy's taxonomy as a way of distinguishing among emphases in aims of discourse, particularly as we examine referential discourse about science in both academic and popular literature. I am identifying the two kinds of writing I am focusing on as "academic and popular referential discourse about science" because I want to emphasize science as the *subject* of the literature under discussion. Kinneavy subdivides referential discourse into three kinds: exploratory (by which he means dialogues, proposals of solutions, and the like); informative (by which he means news articles, textbooks, and reports); and scientific (by which he means "proving a point by arguing from accepted premises" or "proving a point by generalizing about particulars" or "a combination of both").[3] He distinguishes between exploratory discourse and scientific discourse by describing the first as following the logic of *discovery*, as in an essay by Montaigne, and the second as following the logic of *demonstration*, as in a technical report or scientific proof. " 'Demonstration,' in this sense, is synonymous with 'confirmation and justification.' "[4] But Kinneavy himself breaks down the subdivisions by immediately declaring that technical writing is both informative and scientific. I would prefer to make my own distinctions about referential discourse.

Academic science writing is referential discourse which focuses so specifically on the presentation of its subject—the logos of the communication—that the rhetorical elements of ethos and pathos are de-emphasized and, to some degree, standardized. The ethos of most academic science writing is uniform and non-individualized. The persona, which is usually implied and seldom made explicit, is that of someone dedicated to the scientific method—observation, hypothesis formation, hypothesis verification, analysis—and comfortable with the formulaic presentation of research—introduction, research design, research results, analysis. The format of academic science writing is as rigid a literary product as a sonnet and restricts the development of ethos and pathos as it facilitates the development of the logos. Since a technical audience always has limited and formulaic expectations of any technical communication, the presentation of the logos almost simultaneously establishes the ethos and pathos of the discourse. Academic science writing is limited in its rhetorical development by the dialectical nature of each piece of scientific discourse, which is both a response to a past assertion and, at the same time, a further assertion inviting a future response; each is only a single interchange in a continual, multifaceted dialogue among specialists in a scientific community.

Popular science writing, however, is not part of an interminable scientific dialectic, and the rhetorical situation is not the same as it is for academic science writing. For one thing, the audience is different. Rather than addressing a scientific community, it addresses a lay community of non-scientific or limited scientific background, and the possibilities of pathetic appeal are considerably broader. For another thing, in popular science the persona of the author may be quite different from the academic science persona. It may be more relaxed, more informal, more reassuring, or perhaps more imaginative or more expressive. It may even be non-scientific altogether, as when journalists or lay-people attempt to synthesize scholarly work for presentation to a lay audience, as Peter Farb did in *Word Play* or John McPhee did in *Basin and Range*. The possibilities of ethical appeal are also considerably broader.

Some indication of the difference between academic and popular science writing can be garnered by comparing examples from each kind of discourse. The academic science sample is taken from a professional journal and follows a prescribed format, presenting first an abstract of the article and then beginning the article itself with a clearly delineated introduction; the separate parts of the article are indicated throughout by subheadings, including the section of conclusions. Clearly the textual format of the article indicates its content more than its content decides its form.

The first five sentences of the abstract read:

The eddy diffusion coefficient is estimated as a function of altitude, separately for the Jovian troposphere and mesosphere. The growth-rate and motion of particles is estimated for various substances: the water clouds are probably nucleated by $NH_4Cl$, and sodium compounds are likely to be absent at and above the levels of the water clouds. Complex organic molecules produced by the $L\alpha$ photolysis of methane may possibly be the absorbers in the lower mesosphere which account for the low reflectivity of Jupiter in the near-ultraviolet. The optical frequency chromospheres are localized at or just below the Jovian tropopause.[5]

Such a passage is obviously intended for a limited academic audience by a writer representing himself as an academic also. Since the abstract condenses the content of the article, it amplifies its technicality to some degree, yet its terminology is the essential language of the article, and its referential aim is made clear by the abundance of passive constructions and the absence of judgmental terms—other than the words "probably" and "likely," the preponderance of the text consists of words with rather specific denotations.

The opening passage to a chapter in a popular science book presents a completely different sense of the rhetorical possibilities open to its author.

The planet Venus floats, serene and lovely, in the sky of Earth, a bright pin-point of yellowish-white light. Seen or photographed through a telescope, a featureless disc is discerned; a vast unbroken and enigmatic cloud layer shields the surface from our view. No human eye has ever seen the ground of our nearest planetary neighbor.

But we know a great deal about Venus. From radio telescope and space-vehicle observations, we know that the surface temperature is about 900 degrees Fahrenheit. The atmospheric pressure at the surface of Venus is about ninety times that which we experience at the surface of the earth. Since the planet's gravity is about as strong as the Earth's, there are ninety times more molecules in the atmosphere of Venus as in the atmosphere of Earth. This dense atmosphere acts as a kind of insulating blanket, keeping the surface hot through the greenhouse effect and smoothing out temperature differences from place to place.[6]

This passage is far more immediately and more universally comprehended than that of the academic passage, due largely to the dearth of technical terms, the more leisurely pace at which information is dispensed, and the use of metaphorical language. While the sentences are as declarative and as simple as those in the first example, the second example has more active verbs, more colorful adjectives, more imagery, and less specificity of referents. The final sentence, with the use of words like "insulating blanket," "greenhouse," and "smoothing," is both evocative and non-specific. The persona is that of a confident and knowledgeable person who attempts through images and generalities to help lay readers to understand the circumstances of Venus' atmosphere.

In academic and popular science writing, the expectations of both writer and reader must be different, even if the reality, the subject, is essentially the same. While the rhetorical situation invites emphasis on the presentation of evidence in academic referential discourse, it limits emphasis on presentation of evidence in popular referential discourse, because strict denotation is insufficient to represent the reality to a popular audience and connotation-laden figurative language broadens the impact of ethos and pathos. Thus a scientific writer has to shift his approach according to the rhetorical situation if he is to communicate with both academic and popular audiences. In the examples under consideration, the author has made that shift—the first quote is from "Particles, Environments, and Possible Ecologies in the Jovian Atmosphere" by Carl Sagan and E. E. Salpeter, published in the *Astrophysical Journal Supplement*; the second is from "Venus Is Hell," a chapter in *The Cosmic Connection*, written by Carl Sagan and produced by Jerome Agel.

Both passages are examples of referential discourse in the sense that they attempt to explain a scientific context to an interested audience, but they have different intentions. The academic science passage is really an attempt to convince a specialized audience of a scholarly conclusion—what Kinneavy calls "proving a point"—thus demonstrating that scientific discourse is clearly both referential and persuasive at the same time. The popular science passage is an attempt to inform a lay audience of scholarly information that the author assumes to be a professional given; in Kinneavy's taxonomy this is referential discourse with an informative aim. The rigid control over terminology and form in the academic article gives it a specificity of interpretation that is impossible in the popular article; it persuades by the logic of its references. The more the popular author attempts to make clear by analogy, allusion, metaphor, and example, the more he draws upon interpretive expressive language coloring the understanding of the reader and his response, and the less referential the article becomes.

Academic science writing is principally written according to a rhetoric of justification—that is, according to an agreed-upon design for verifying the validity of a hypothesis. "Justification" is an act essential only when there is doubt; it is clearly a persuasive act. But popular science writing is not that restricted; it can be a book of justification—Rachel Carson's *Silent Spring*, for example—or a book of speculation, like Lewis Thomas' *Lives of a Cell*.

To some degree what I am calling "speculation" is what Kinneavy calls "exploratory discourse," the logic of discovery, but I want to use the term strictly in regard to writing about science, particularly the establishment and defense of a hypothesis for which verifying data is still insufficient. In the dialectic of academic science, there is a speculative dimension, but the point of publication is to confirm findings; yet in science generally the freedom to speculate, to devise theories and suggest future findings, is important in helping to establish where to look and what to look for in research.

The moment a writer turns his attention to speculation, to imagining a solution to a problem or proposing a hypothesis which has little chance of verification, the rhetorical problem changes. For a scientist the movement from justification to speculation should nonetheless entail as much of a referential perspective as possible. James Trefil's model of the relationship among areas of scientific inquiry illustrates the difference between the rhetoric of justification and the rhetoric of speculation:

One can visualize the situation in science in terms of concentric circles: At the *center* is that body of time-tested, universally accepted ideas that are set forth in school and college texts. The first circle out from the center is the *frontier*, which interacts constantly with the center, feeding it new ideas that the center, after lengthy testing, adopts and assimilates.

If we move beyond the frontier region of science, however, we come to a hazy outer circle that I like to call the *fringe*. The fringe is characterized by a scarcity of hard data and by a general fuzziness of ideas that make the average scientist very uncomfortable. It is a zone in which neither accepted scientific writ nor reasonable extrapolations of scientific knowledge seem to apply. . . . Yet the fringe has its uses, for it feeds ideas to the frontier.[7]

Trefil emphasizes that, of the ideas in both the fringe and the frontier, "the soundest, most useful of them keep gravitating inward, ring by ring, toward the orthodox center." One of his examples of an idea moving from the fringe to the frontier is the idea of communication with extraterrestrial intelligences, and he cites the germ theory of disease and the theory of continental drift as ideas considered too fringy to merit attention when they were first introduced. While centrist ideas are the topic of most academic science writing and frontier ideas may find some academic as well as popular audiences, the topics of the fringe have been the sole province of popular science writing directed at a lay audience and heavily promoted by entrepreneurial publishing houses. While centrist ideas are chiefly justification, frontier and fringe ideas are chiefly speculation—a frontier subject only gets to justify itself when it is close to the center.

Some indications of the nature of the rhetoric of speculation, including its basic elements and its differentiating features, can be gained by examining popular science writing on extraterrestrial intelligence, including extraterrestrial visitations to Earth. Thanks largely to the success of Erich von Däniken, there is an enormous body of popular literature devoted to verifying the existence in ancient times of spacemen on the planet Earth, including von Däniken's own series of books and a host of imitators.[8] Most of these repeat or enlarge upon a rather limited number of ideas, all questioning academic archaelogy and astronomy and arguing from the evidence of ancient artifacts that extraterrestrial lifeforms landed on Earth eons ago and influenced the evolution of mankind and/or the development of its civilizations.

Such mass-produced theorizing conflicts with frontier research into the existence of extraterrestrial intelligence, an idea given much and vocal credence by a number of prominent scientists, because it links an idea for which there is frontier support with one for which there is only fringe support. Not surprisingly, there has been a backlash, including a number of attacks on von Däniken.[9]

Yet von Däniken's books conform in many ways to the kind of rhetoric of speculation used by orthodox scientists to explore frontier topics, and rhetorically speaking, popular literature makes little distinction between science and what the academic community calls "pseudoscience." Because scientific discourse is chiefly referential, the deciding factor is often evidence to which the popular reader has no access and by which he is often befuddled, particularly when both protagonist and antagonist tend to speak the same language.

In the rhetoric of speculation the author usually presents himself as an underdog. Erich von Däniken writes in his introduction:

It took courage to write this book and it will take courage to read it. Because its theories and proofs do not fit into the mosaic of traditional archaeology, constructed so laboriously and firmly cemented down, scholars will call it nonsense and put it on the Index of those books which are better left unmentioned. Laymen will withdraw into the snail shell of their familiar world when faced with the probability that finding out about our past will be even more mysterious and adventurous than finding out about our future.[10]

Throughout the book he represents himself as an iconoclast daring to defy the academic establishment, whom he represents as being unimaginative and corrupt:

Scholars make things very easy for themselves. They stick a couple of old potsherds together, search for one or two adjacent cultures, stick a label on the restored find, and—hey, presto!—once again everything fits splendidly into the approved pattern of thought. This method is obviously very much simpler than chancing the idea that an embarrassing technical skill might have existed or the thought of space travelers in the distant past. That would be complicating matters unnecessarily.[11]

Such statements embody von Däniken's ethical and pathetic appeal. The pose not only creates an image of von Däniken in the reader's mind and engenders sympathy for him, but it also plays upon the reader's distrust of the scientific establishment. Von Däniken and the reader are conspiring to overthrow the stuffy, pompous, elitist academicians who dismiss the kind of "scientific speculation" that von Däniken engages in.

Continually von Däniken presents himself as the voice of common sense. In regard to a Saharan wall painting he writes:

"Without overstretching my imagination I got the impression that the great god Mars is depicted in a space or diving suit."[12] Or he says, "Seen from the air, the clear-cut impression that the 37-mile-long plain of Nazca made on *me* was that of an airfield!"[13] About a stone relief from Palenque he writes, "There sits a human being, with the upper part of his body bent forward like a racing motorcyclist; today any child would identify his vehicle as a rocket."[14] The implication of such remarks is that comprehension is available to the average reader without specialized knowledge and that academic credentials only get in the way of the truth.

The need for self-justification is strong in the rhetoric of speculation. Ronald Story's attack on von Däniken opens with both a defense of its writing and an attack on the scientific establishment which has allowed von Däniken to flourish:

The academic community has pretty much taken the attitude that the theory of ancient astronauts is beneath the dignity of serious investigators even to consider. The whole idea, they feel, is simply nonsense from the beginning. Why spend valuable professional time on a subject so obviously absurd when there are more important things to do?

Story then quotes a call to arms against pseudoscience by Philip Abelson and responds to it:

But how do we find truth if no one will help us? The complacency of most academicians closes them off as a source of information. The high schools and elementary schools are doing little more than the colleges in combatting the pseudosciences. . . . And so the pseudosciences go largely unexamined and continue to flourish. It is my hope that this book will provide an antidote to one pseudoscience—that popularized by Erich von Däniken.[15]

By and large Story's book does provide an antidote, but it also imitates von Däniken's tone throughout—skeptical, suspicious, sarcastic, argumentative. The ethos of an intelligent man outraged by fraud and deception is very similar to the ethos evoked by von Däniken, of an intelligent man provoked by the timidity and lack of imagination of the scientific community. The appeal to the audience is very much the same—identifying the readers as people too intelligent, too perceptive to be misled, and also as people unsympathetic to the academic community.

The rhetoric of speculation to some degree demands an adversarial relationship with the mainstream scientific community. Witness the introduction to the book *The Cosmic Connection* by Carl Sagan:

After centuries of muddy surmise, unfettered speculation, stodgy conservatism, and unimaginative disinterest, the subject of extraterrestrial life has finally come of age. It has now reached a practical stage where it can be pursued by rigorous scientific techniques, where it has achieved scientific respectability, and where its significance is widely understood. Extraterrestrial life is an idea whose time has come. . . .

The astronomical discoveries we are in the midst of making are of the broadest human significance. If this book plays a small role in broadening public consideration of these exploratory ventures, it will have served its purpose.[16]

This is exactly the kind of position von Däniken takes in the opening chapter of *Chariots of the Gods?*:

The time has come for us to admit our insignificance by making discoveries in the infinite unexplored cosmos. Only then shall we realize that we are nothing but ants in the vast state of the universe. And yet our future and our opportunities lie in the universe, where the gods promised they would.

Not until we have taken a look into the future shall we be strong enough and bold enough to investigate our past honestly.[17]

The attitudes toward those in the center of the scientific community who have held back research on the area each author purposes to explore is virtually identical. As von Däniken continually intercepts the argument against him that he is not a scholar by proclaiming it throughout the book, Sagan too justifies himself for dealing with material about which little has been proven:

Part Three is devoted to the possibility of communicating with extraterrestrial intelligence on planets of other stars. Since no such contact has yet been made—our efforts to date have been feeble—this section is necessarily speculative. I have not hesitated to speculate within what I perceive to be the bounds of scientific plausibility. And although I am not by training a philosopher or sociologist or historian, I have not hesitated to draw philosophical or social or historical implications of astronomy or space explorations. . . .

As with all ongoing work and especially all speculative subjects, some of the statements in these pages will elicit vigorous demurrers. . . . But I believe that the more controversial opinions expressed here have, nevertheless, a significant scientific constituency.[18]

Both von Däniken and Sagan present themselves as figures attempting to cut through the stagnation and trepidation of centrist science.

The rhetoric of speculation by its nature allows greater freedom to the imagination and both von Däniken and Sagan feel free to draw on it. We have already seen von Däniken using intuitive responses as testimony, but he is also capable of creating a fanciful picture. Chapter Two of *Chariots of the Gods?*, for example, describes an imaginary journey by spaceship to the planet Earth; Carl Sagan's highly successful book and television series *Cosmos* repeatedly uses what the author calls a "spaceship of the imagination" to dramatize experiences as yet unproven.[19] The gift of imagination is one of the spurs to the speculative mind. Both as popular science writers and as speculators, the authors of both books draw upon a desire to make the reader see and experience as well as read. But when Sagan writes in *The Cosmic Connection*,

In the Book of Judges there is an account of a slain lion discovered to be infested by a hive of bees, a strange and apparently pointless incident. But the constellation of Leo in the night sky is adjacent to a cluster of stars, visible on a clear night as a fuzzy patch of light, called Praesepe. From its telescopic appearance, modern astronomers call it "The Beehive." I wonder if an image of Praesepe, obtained by one man of exceptional eyesight, in days before the telescope, has been preserved for us in the Book of Judges.[20]

we have to recognize that his imagination is getting the best of his judgment. The same thing happens to von Däniken when he writes:

When passing cattle shook and threatened to overturn the Ark of the Covenant, Uzzah grabbed hold of it. He fell dead on the spot, as if struck by lightning.

> Undoubtedly the Ark was electrically charged! If we reconstruct it today according to the instructions handed down by Moses, an electric conductor of several hundred volts is produced. . . . Without actually consulting Exodus, I seem to remember that the Ark was often surrounded by flashing sparks and that Moses made use of this "transmitter" whenever he needed help and advice.[21]

In fact, both men are wrong and both are distorting the Bible to make a biased case for their own imaginative worldviews.

In order to make the case that the lion and beehive story in the Book of Judges is evidence of a Biblical astronomical record, Sagan feels obliged to negate the Biblical story. In other words, if it has no other meaning, then Sagan's explanation will seem all the more plausible. But of course it has a meaning—Samson, who has killed the lion with his bare hands, discovers the beehive and invents a riddle: "Out of the eater came something to eat, Out of the strong came something sweet" (Judges 14:18).[22] The solving of the riddle has a number of ramifications in the life of Samson and in the relationship between Israelites and Philistines—it is not a "strange and pointless incident." If we are to imagine a record of discovery, why not the discovery of a beehive in the carcass of a lion?

Von Däniken's memory of the Ark is equally suspicious. It's rather odd that he deliberately announces that he hasn't checked the text because a quick reading of Exodus 36–40, the concluding chapters of the book, reveals the instructions for making not only the Ark, described as a "chest of acacia-wood" (Exodus 37:1), but the whole of the Tabernacle of the Tent of the Presence and what happened there. At no time is it surrounded by flashing sparks and clearly it is supposed that Yahweh himself visited it, at which time "Moses was unable to enter the Tent of the Presence, because the cloud had settled on it and the glory of the Lord filled the Tabernacle" (Exodus 4:35).

The rhetoric of speculation demands a controversy, a persona that is combative and imaginative, and an invitation to the reader to be responsive to flights of fancy and skeptical of conservative science. In these matters it seems as if speculative pseudoscience and speculative science have little to distinguish them, although a close reading of both books would reveal that von Däniken's flights of fancy are far more typical. The unsupported assertion and the imaginative recreation which never circles back and anchors itself to well-documented evidence are constants of his writing. With Sagan the fanciful flights come off more often as moments of exuberance—one thing Sagan conveys that von Däniken can't is a love of science, a sense of wonder about the universe that turns his fancy toward spirited play; von Däniken can't play.

Yet both men influence their readers by the presentation of ideas through imagination and ultimately it is in the logos of the presentation that the realms of fringe and frontier science establish clear borderlines. Take as a comparative item their examination of the moons of Mars.

Von Däniken gives a little history of the discovery of the Martian moons, Phobos and Deimos, highlighting what he takes to be the strange references to them in *Gulliver's Travels* and elsewhere before their official discovery in 1877, and then dismisses the idea that they are captured asteroids. He then attempts to prove that Phobos and Deimos are artificial moons launched into space by an ancient, highly technical civilization on Mars by reference to the book, *Intelligent Life in the Universe* (1966) co-authored by I. S. Shklovskii and Carl Sagan. Von Däniken writes that

As a result of a series of measurements, Sagan came to the conclusion that Phobos must be hollow and a hollow moon cannot be natural.

In fact, the peculiarities of Phobos' orbit bear no relation to its apparent mass, whereas such orbits are typical in the case of hollow bodies.[23]

On the surface this seems a reliable statement. Its use of authority is one which is easily identifiable—certainly Sagan is the best-known astronomer in the world, and the mere citation of a source makes an assertion seem verifiable. By mentioning a separate work of Shklovskii's elsewhere in the chapter, von Däniken gives himself the appearance of being well versed in the subject.

In fact, much of the discussion of the moons of Mars in *Char-*

*iots of the Gods?* seems taken from *Intelligent Life in the Universe*. Shklovskii and Sagan open the chapter with a reference to *Gulliver's Travels* and the identical quote from the section on Laputa (von Däniken's is longer), but the two astronomers also explain how Jonathan Swift could have known about the moons; von Däniken prefers to suggest a mystery. There are other parallels as well.[24] But the astronomers give a great deal more detail, including an account of the observations and conclusions of the astronomer B. P. Sharpless, whose findings are the basis for Shklovskii's theory that the moon Phobos may be hollow and therefore artificial. Yet toward the end of the chapter, they quote extensively from a fellow scientist who doubts the accuracy of Sharpless' findings and then they themselves add:

It is possible that Sharpless' results are incorrect. In this case, the hypothesis that Phobos and Deimos have an artificial origin would lose its scientific support. Only when new and very precise observations are carried out will we be able either to disprove or verify Sharpless' results. . . .

Even if future observations indicate that the reported secular acceleration of Phobos is spurious, the hypothesis that the moons of Mars are of artificial origin has nevertheless been provocative, and thereby served a useful purpose.[25]

Shklovskii himself thus points out the possible error of his own theory. The presentation of speculation among scientists does not allow for making unsubstantiated claims as if they were substantiated facts; the science-based popular science books continually make that distinction—the pseudoscience books tend not to.

But the presentation of logos in the examples of von Däniken and Sagan reveals another element of the rhetoric of speculation. At the close of his discussion of Phobos, von Däniken treats Shklovskii's theory as a proof of an ancient technological civilization on Mars and turns his speculations toward increasingly unanswerable questions.

If the view supported by reputable scientists East and West that Mars once had an advanced civilization is correct, the question arises: Why does it no longer exist today? Did the intelligences on Mars have to seek a new environment? Did their home planet, which was losing more and more oxygen, force them to look for new territories to settle? Was a cosmic catastrophe responsible for the downfall of the civilization? Lastly, were some of the inhabitants of Mars able to escape to a neighboring planet?[26]

None of these questions grows organically from the discussion of the moons of Mars but rather systematically creates a scenario which assumes a host of preconceptions about the planet. Note that one fantastic question, about the loss of oxygen, has no relevance to the discussion and would seem derived from thin air if we didn't known that Shklovskii and Sagan make mention of the John Carter of Mars series of science-fiction novels by Edgar Rice Burroughs, in which the danger of loss of oxygen threatens to wipe out life on the planet. Note also that none of the questions actually posits a series of alternatives but instead only leads the reader deeper into von Däniken's theory.

But a similar discussion of the moons of Mars in Sagan's *The Cosmic Connection* leads to two different kinds of speculation. Commenting on the photographic evidence of Mariner 9, Sagan writes:

Phobos appears to be an entirely natural fragment of a larger rock severely battered by repeated collisions; holes have been dug, pieces have been chipped off. It looks a little like the hand axes, chipped along natural fracture planes, made by our Pleistocene ancestors. There is no sign of technology on it. Phobos is not an artificial satellite.[27]

This report of the scientific evidence restores some of Sagan's credibility since it refutes a possible proof of a theory Sagan would like to believe. On the heels of this passage of informative discourse, he almost immediately speculates:

I believe we are looking at the end product of a kind of collisional natural selection, in which fragments have been broken off from a larger parent body, and we are seeing only the two pieces, Phobos and Deimos, that remain.[28]

This is the kind of scientific speculation which arises from the examination of a reality and then posits an explanation. It is precisely the kind of speculation that advances science because it is a hypothesis drawn from evidence awaiting either confirmation or denial.

However, once Sagan has described the pull of gravity on Phobos as "about one one-thousandth of that on Earth," he proceeds to another kind of speculation:

The velocity necessary to launch an object into orbit about Phobos is only twenty miles an hour. An amateur baseball pitcher could easily launch a baseball into orbit around Phobos.[29]

Sagan expands on this image in a half dozen ways in the next paragraph, but his speculations here are different from those on the origin of the planet; they amusingly illustrate the significance of low gravity in a very graphic and concrete way. Thus when Sagan says later that "these sports possibilities may, one day a century or so hence, provide a tourist industry for Phobos and Deimos," he is being wry, and the cautious reader will know enough to back off this speculation, not to take it seriously, especially when it is coupled with the statement that follows it: "But baseball on Phobos is no more an argument for going there than, to take a random example, golf is for going to the moon."[30] It is a segue into another subject and a slap in passing at the astronaut who hit a golfball on the moon. Speculative language is more complex in Sagan because he utilizes its full range.

Judgment about the validity of any scientific discourse demands close scrutiny of its logos. In the dialectic of academic science that scrutiny is constantly forthcoming, it is the lifeblood of academic publishing and discussion. But the rhetoric of popular science writing undergoes no such close examination, and the lay reader has only rhetorical analysis to estimate the sincerity and validity of the argument presented. Yet, just as a scientist can divide areas of scientific inquiry according to their current demonstrable validity into center, frontier, and fringe, so the rhetorician can divide referential discourse about science according to rhetorical situation into the rhetoric of justification and the rhetoric of speculation and can use the elements of speculative rhetoric as a means of estimating the reliability of the logos under analysis.

Plato objected to rhetoric on the grounds that it allowed people to argue convincingly the worst case; he preferred dialectic
and pretended that that was what his dialogues displayed. While
it is true that there is no greater weapon against outright fraud
than a secure knowledge of the truth, in works that use the
rhetoric of speculation, a rhetorical analysis of their ethos, pathos, and logos will go a long way toward establishing the reliability of the structure of their argument and, perhaps even
more, the willingness of their authors to keep the rhetoric of
justification separate from the rhetoric of speculation.

# 8

# The Rhetoric of Opinion: Advocacy, Public Affairs, and Logic

In his *Rhetoric* Aristotle says this about the kinds of rhetoric:

Rhetoric falls into three divisions, determined by the three classes of listeners to speeches. For of the three elements in speech-making—speaker, subject, and person addressed—it is the last one, the hearer, that determines the speech's end and object. The hearer must be either a judge, with a decision to make about things past or future, or an observer. A member of the assembly decides about future events, a juryman about past events; while those who merely decide on the orator's skill are observers. From this it follows that there are three divisions of oratory—(1) political, (2) forensic, and (3) the ceremonial oratory of display.[1]

Other translators term political oratory as deliberative or advisory, forensic as legal or judicial, and ceremonial as epideictic.[2] In essense, Aristotle is distinguishing among audiences that would include members of a legislative body, members of a law court, and spectators at a ceremonial occasion; the study of rhetoric was originally an outgrowth of specific occasions for public oratory.

As this book has already demonstrated, these categories are far too few. Rhetoric may be divided into as many different divisions as there are occasions for discourse; even the kinds of advocacy practiced in modern discourse are varied in intent and function. Nonetheless, Aristotle's description of the divisions of rhetoric is useful here as we consider one particular branch of advocacy, the political column.

Aristotle goes on to make further distinctions:

> Political speaking urges us either to do or not to do something: one of these two courses is always taken by private counsellors, as well as by men who address public assemblies. Forensic speaking either attacks or defends somebody: one or other of these two things must always be done by the parties in a case. The ceremonial oratory of display either praises or censures somebody. . . .
>
> Rhetoric has three distinct ends in view, one for each of its three kinds. The political orator aims at establishing the expediency or the harmfulness of a proposed course of action; if he urges its acceptance, he does so on the ground that it will do good; if he urges its rejection, he does so on the ground that it will do harm; and all other points, such as whether the proposal is just or unjust, honourable or dishonourable, he brings in as subsidiary and relative to this main consideration.[3]

For Aristotle, the practical application of rhetoric in the public arena is far more limited than the modern rhetorician would view it, and the political columnist, while he may engage in political or deliberative rhetoric of a nature much as Aristotle describes it, is really not as constrained in options as the political orator might be. In addition to attempting to establish the "expediency or harmfulness" of specific actions, he may speculate about options without adopting a specific position, and his considerations of political issues may not extend so far as to propose specific courses of action. Aristotle's deliberative speaker (and the modern assemblyman, as well) is usually engaged in deciding the merits of particular laws; the political columnist has a much broader sphere in which to move and his audience is equally broad and heterogeneous. While he is surely a deliberative rhetorician, the political columnist needs to conform to the demands of a different mode of deliberative rhetoric than that in which the politician operates.

The rhetoric of opinion, then, is initially influenced by the constraints of mode. The columnist's task is not necessarily to advocate specific actions or formulate specific regulations but instead to speculate on current issues and ideas. Richard Reeves has written that "a column, usually, is one idea expanded."[4] Similarly Tom Wicker, in his book, *On Press*, writes:

An opinion column needs an *idea*—rarely more than one, given length restrictions—whether complex or simple, original or conventional. In journalism as in any other form, an idea does not require acceptance to justify its existence; nor does it necessarily exist to achieve anything other than an intellectual end. An idea *is*; and an informed, opinionated, argumentative person—all of which an opinion columnist must be—will put forward ideas, defend them, modify or abandon them, attack or analyze or even accept those of others, as *concepts*, intellectual speculations, without regard to their general popularity or immediate utility or relevance to a given situation. An idea in itself is of interest, and offering ideas is the task of the opinion columnist at his infrequent best.[5]

Elsewhere in the same book Wicker summarizes his position thus: "ideas always challenge assumptions, not necessarily successfully, and that may be as good a description as any— 'challenging assumptions'—for the work of the opinion columnist."[6]

These remarks suggest that the nature of the political column is more amorphous than that of the political address, that its purpose is, more often than not, less clear-cut, less tangible, less concrete. Nevertheless, because it expresses opinion and often attempts to validate that opinion as well as speculate about it, the political column is chiefly a form of deliberative rhetoric.

Classical rhetoricians divided rhetoric into five parts: invention, arrangement, style, memory, and delivery. The last two have been principally the province of oratory, although if we consider delivery to include performance or presentation, it is certainly relevant to all the kinds of rhetoric we have been considering in this book. In earlier chapters we have considered arrangement and style as they have been reflected in the ethos, pathos, and logos of various forms of discourse. But because in some way they help to explain the forces which produce the political column, in dealing with the rhetoric of opinion we need to understand something about invention and arrangement as they apply to the composition of the column. Invention is primarily the discovery of information and lines of argument con-

cerning a given topic, and arrangement is primarily the ordering of that information in the most effective way. Professional
columnists of almost any type have similar ways of handling
the tasks of invention and arrangement.

To begin with, professional columnists are constantly in search
of ideas to write about and continually aware of the field in
which they are working. Richard Reeves says of his writing,

I keep manila envelopes that I keep stuffing things into which might
lead to future columns. At points where it seems advisable I'll flip
through there and out of twenty notes to myself or clippings, my guess
is that one out of four—might even be less than that—eventually becomes a column.[7]

Tom Wicker keeps a similar collection of material.[8] Like other
political columnists, both men draw upon such resources when
something new in public events connects with something in
the past. As Wicker says,

political reporters should be, and most are, assiduous "string-savers."
Some quote not apropos in today's story may be just right for next
week's; or some note jotted down on one story may mesh with another from a second story to make still a third.[9]

To some extent, then, the political columnist depends upon
current events and connections in his own mind to create the
column. His role is chiefly responsive, interpretative, and speculative, and his advocacy is often limited by the narrow focus
on immediate events and by the constraints of his forum, a
column of some 700 to 1200 words. These constraints make it
important that the column express one idea at a time rather
than a panoply of ideas—there is simply no room for development or substantiation if the subject is too broad or too complex. It also means that the column is not apt to be an elaborate
brief for a specific cause or issue without currency in public
affairs; it is usually only after politicians of one kind or another
have generated the issue that the opinion columnists discuss
it.

With these kinds of restraints upon the columnist's "invention," the material for a column is generated and arranged for

presentation. The arrangement is governed in part by the limitations of space and in part by the specific slant the columnist brings to the subject—the examples he wants to use, the emphasis he wants to make. The reader's task is to interpret the argument the columnist makes and to decide whether to accept, reject, or ignore it. Influencing the reader's response will be the writer's use of ethos, pathos, and logos, the distinguishing elements of the arguments.

To give a sense of ethos in the rhetoric of opinion, we need to examine several different columnnists, all of them writing about the same general topic, the election of 1984, in which Republican incumbent Ronald Reagan won a landslide victory over Democratic candidate Walter Mondale. For example, Lars-Erik Nelson opens his column this way:

Ready to pay the mystery tax? Ready to feel the mystery ax? Ready to sail into the Twilight Zone?

For the first time in American history, the nation has re-elected an incumbent president whose specific economic, foreign and military policies are more of a question mark than those of his challenger.[10]

The edge to the flippant opening of this column suggests a scornful persona, contemptuous of the election results and the policies of the incumbent. While the body of the piece offers arguments of the necessity for Reagan to do things he has pledged not to do, the column concludes with a scornful tone:

Reagan sold the electorate exciting magic potions: Pay the deficit by economic growth and a balanced-budget amendment to the Constitution. If that works, then there's no need to raise taxes or cut any federal spending. Prevent nuclear war by investing in a magic bulletproof shield—and give it to Russia.

If nothing else, the second Reagan term will be an adventure into the unknown.

The ethos voices anger at the election results and attempts to generate fear about what those results signify, which is an attractive persona for those upset about the results.

By contrast, Anthony Lewis's column presents a more controlled, more reasonable persona:

It is going to be a different country.

The size of President Reagan's victory stunned even those who had anticipated it, but I wonder how many people understand what it may bring by way of lasting changes in American politics and law and social conditions.

We are not used to ideological politicians in this country. Most Reagan voters were probably motivated less by ideology than by economics, liking for the man, patriotic feelings associated with him. But ideology is what we are going to get.[11]

In particular the opening sentence and the final sentence of the third paragraph are somber declarations that suggest a person disturbed by the outcome of the election, and the tone of the piece is generally ominous, as the conclusion makes clear:

The consolation, for those of us who care about civil liberties and social justice and an end to the arms race, is to remember that there are cycles in politics. We elected Harding and Coolidge and Hoover, but we survived the empty greed of the 1920's. The only thing is that survival is trickier now.

The conclusion makes clear the position that the author takes on several political issues; more importantly, it conveys a sense of foreboding and gloom—the consolation doesn't seem to console the author very much and probably is not meant to console the reader who shares Lewis's sense of foreboding.

From these two columns one can sense that the authors are politically aligned—they are both discouraged by the election results and worried about its effects on similar issues—but the personae they present are markedly different and will affect readers differently.

The appeals being made to the audience, the pathos in each column, are also different. James J. Kilpatrick, who responds favorably to the election, continually plays upon the affection of the reader for the incumbent by expressing it early on—"With one voice, nearly 60 percent of the voters joined in a resounding chorus: Can't help loving that Ron of mine"—and continuing to speak affectionately of the President throughout—"We saw the old Gipper, with Nancy at his side, smiling his way through a forest of flags"; "He offered himself, the lines in his face a little deeper, the hair a little grayer, the bum ear a little deafer." In such phrases he generates sympathy and fondness, and his conclusion is glowing in the image it creates—"It suffices for the moment for the president to savor the sweet taste of a triumph well won."[12]

In contrast, both Lewis and Nelson try to discourage the reader and perhaps cause him to regret the results of the election; however, there are subtle differences in the kinds of pathos each writer attempts to create. Lewis plays on our fear with such images as that of conservatives Jerry Falwell and Jesse Helms arguing that "they played a large part in mobilizing the soldiers of this victory, and they are going to demand their share of the spoils."[13] The metaphor is deliberately that of conquest rather than democratic election, and the image engenders both a sense of helplessness at the feet of the conquerors and a sense of anger at their motives. Nelson, on the other hand, continually tries to alarm us about the uncertainty of the future by referring to mysteries and inevitabilities, and to engender in the reader something of the scorn expressed by the persona of the column.

The elements of ethos and pathos are naturally a measurable part of these columns, but their chief appeal has to come from logos. Each column, if it presents only one idea, has to either substantiate it in a way that seems logical or to divert the reader from the lack of substantiation. But the argument is not necessarily an attempt to arrive at a specific point; it may also be an attempt to create a mood or attitude or evoke a feeling.

For example, in the piece by Kilpatrick, the generation of affectionate attitudes toward the president is the central concern of the article; it begins and ends on a note of triumph and attempts to downplay any larger significance to the election than the popularity of the president. Such a restrained view adds credence to Kilpatrick's ethos, of course, and adds to the pathetic appeal to complacency about the election results. Most of the negative remarks—about public indifference to Walter Mondale's positions, about the need for the Democratic Party to recognize the insignificance of minority interest and the importance of majority desires—are directed at Reagan's opposition, and the concerns that are so important to Lewis and Nelson—the deficit, the likelihood of a tax increase, the shakiness of foreign policy—are skipped over. All Kilpatrick says of the tax increase is, "Except for his promise not to seek an increase in taxes—a promise he will have to wiggle gently out of—Reagan made no promises at all."[14] Kilpatrick's distribution of weight to various issues—his arrangement of his argument—tends to reinforce his view that we should all be content with Reagan's victory.

In Nelson's column, understandably, the possible tax increase takes a more prominent position. The opening sentence—"Ready to pay the mystery tax?"—establishes the likelihood of a tax increase as a major point in this article. Nelson then establishes as his general introduction the idea that "the problems are there; the only mysteries are when Reagan will accept that they are real and how he will respond." The first major section of the substantiation for this view is an argument about the deficit, including a digression comparing "how angry *we all* were at abuses in the $13 billion food stamp program" (my italics) with an implication about how angry we all ought to feel about $17 billion in interest annually being paid on the deficit, the money going not "to the black woman in front of you in the checkout line" but to banks—"the beneficiaries are white men in suits." This attention to waste and abuse is another appeal to pathos and slows the development of the logos, which continues with the conclusion that "there will be a tax. Whom it will hit, how much it will be and when it will fall are mysteries." The second section of the substantiation deals more briefly with cuts in federal spending, initiatives on the Middle East, and progress on arms control. The conclusion of the article reminds us that all of this would have been clear with Mondale, and returns to the theme of Reagan's second term as "an adventure into the unknown." Nelson's article is fairly well unified, although the attempts to create pathos detract from the argument. Nonetheless he establishes his point, argues its validity, and returns to his original view, and in this regard his logos is tighter and clearer than Kilpatrick's.[15]

The argument of Lars-Erik Nelson's article on the 1984 election is a fairly standard form of logos—present your position, provide evidence for it, restate your position. Other columnists choose different organizations which suggest different goals as well as different means of arguing.

For example, Tom Wicker's column on the election was virtually two columns, one on the interpretation of the significance of Reagan's victory, and one on the means of achieving the personal victory that the first half of the column concluded it was. Thus the column's parts are tightly linked sequentially, but the argument does not develop uniformly. The first three paragraphs confirm the results of the election and end by asking, "Was something happening other than the re-election of a strongly positioned president over a candidate who miscalculated his campaign?" The second section opens with an answer: "The evidence so far does not suggest—to me, at least—party re-alignment," substantiates that position with data about the election results, and ends with a reference to an alternative explanation for Reagan's victory other than ideology—"his and his managers' mastery of television—the new reality of American politics." The third and largest section analyzes the candidates' use of television and the conclusion of the article grows out of this discussion:

There's no point in deploring or denigrating any of this or wishing television would go away. It won't; the Republicans' use of it was not a perversion of politics but a realization of opportunity; and future candidates in both parties will be learning from the Reagan campaign about how to use it more effectively. They'd better.[16]

One may say of this piece that Wicker creates a relaxed, reliable ethos, continually sounding even-handed and thoughtful by avoiding terms which suggest partisan judgment or emotional response; his voice is always calm and analytical. This is not to say that he is correct in his interpretation, merely that his ethical appeal is far more non-partisan than we've noticed in the other columnists. Yet the logos of the piece is fairly weak in its overall arrangement, if not in its substantiation of individual points, because it seems to change direction halfway through, at the point where he begins to discuss television. In fact, this piece is not "one idea expanded" but two ideas uncomfortably linked by analysis.

If Tom Wicker's analysis of the election results, by its attention to the issue of television, seems to make a more universal
point than the reader initially expects, the column by William
Safire on the same event offers a more carefully crafted but
equally surprizing twist in its logos. Safire begins by raising the
question of the significance of the election, just as others do:

Was the Reagan sweep primarily a personal victory of a popular leader
in prosperous times, like Ike's re-election in 1956?
    If so, all the opposition has to do is hunker down, rebuild its coali-
tion of women, minorities and labor, take advantage of foreign mis-
haps and the certain turn of the business cycle, and choose a telegenic
spokesman in 1988 who can win on the slogan "Time for a Change!"
    Or was the conservative reaffirmation of 1984 a signal that most of
the Republican Party philosophy reflects the beliefs of a growing majority—that the Democratic opposition's appeal for "social fairness"
and foreign accomodation was the voice of the fringe, and led to a
rejection nearly as thorough as the total defeat of Goldwater in 1964
and McGovern in 1972?
    If so—if the 1984 vote was more against a liberal philosophy than a
thank-you to a successful incumbent—then America's ideological center of gravity has been shifting significantly.[17]

It is clear from the way the questions are phrased and the terminology is weighted that Safire will elect to agree with the
second interpretation. These two alternatives continue to be
discussed throughout the article. Safire goes on to argue that
the "consensus will be to characterize the Reagan re-election as
a great personal triumph," as indeed Wicker and Kilpatrick,
among a host of others, do, but that Safire believes that Reagan
won because "he has demonstrated himself to be Mr. Nice
Tough Guy, representing the middle-class's long buried sense
of self-worth and newfound freedom from guilt," a statement
making a pathetic appeal to the readers to feel exactly those
things. Safire suggests that misperceptions of the ideological
significance of the election will help solidify the Republican
party's base in the American majority.
    But the article abruptly turns midway through, not unlike
Wicker's column, to a separate but related issue, the way Reagan should "capitalize on this victory of personal capitalism."

Safire suggests a number of things Reagan should and should not do about taxes and foreign policy and argues that the "prairie fire" Reagan spoke of starting twenty years earlier with Goldwater's campaign

did not whip across the land because of any one man's charm or mastery of prompting devices, nor will it be snuffed out when Mr. Reagan rides off into the sunset. He succeeded in his first term because he understood that the majority wants government to protect our freedom as it leaves us alone, and he will keep the flame burning for his successors by remaining true to that mandate.[18]

The article changes direction by becoming an argument directed not at a reader interested in an interpretation of the election results but indirectly at a reader who has won the election and needs to have the significance of his victory interpreted for him and be reminded of his ideology; perhaps it can assist in keeping the victor on track. At any rate the logos has shifted to an argument on how to stay true to certain ideals after starting out as an argument for the triumph of such ideals and the meaning of certain events.

To some degree, this undercuts Safire's earlier position, that the election results indicate a major ideological shift in the population; if the President and the vast majority of the public are in total agreement about the important issues of the day, why would Safire worry that Reagan might renege on the positions of twenty years standing? Obviously Safire either didn't recognize this contradiction or chose to veil his attempt to influence government by couching it in terms of vindication.

The rhetoric of opinion, then, is often considerably less substantial than other forms of deliberative rhetoric on which stricter demands of logic and evidence are made. By virtue of its mode—the popular newspaper column—and its purpose—to discuss and speculate rather than to legislate and advocate—and also because of the demands of its regular and frequent production, it is often severely limited as deliberative rhetoric. One may also argue that, given the selective responses of readers, it less often persuades the undecided than confirms the position of the converted.

Nonetheless, it demonstrates the universality of rhetoric as a descriptive model for public discourse. In the rhetoric of opinion by which advocates for various ideas and political observers of every stripe speculate, argue, and analyze, the elements of rhetoric may be held to less demanding and precise functions than they were originally held in the legislative, judicial, and ceremonial discourse of the past; but they are nonetheless created in similar ways and illuminated by similar means of analysis.

# Part IV

# RHETORIC AND
# ENTERTAINMENT

# 9

# A Listener's Guide to the Rhetoric of Popular Music

Underlying most of the research into popular music has been the supposition that, somehow, it affects its listeners in subtle and significant ways and therefore ought to be studied and analyzed. However, the small body of research on popular music that has been done has chiefly demonstrated the difficulty of such study and analysis and the diversity of approaches available to do it. David Reisman outlined some of those difficulties in an early article, concluding that:

one cannot hope to understand the influence of any one medium, say music, without an understanding of the total character structure of a person. . . . Plainly, we cannot simply ask "Who listens to what?" before we find out who "who" is and what "what" is by means of a psychological and content analysis of the manifold uses, the plasticity of music for its variegated audiences.[1]

By and large, these are the questions that researchers have been asking ever since, and slowly, incrementally, we have developed a sense of who the audience is and what the thing is they listen to. Research has focused on both content analysis of songs and also examinations of their audiences' conscious and self-conscious reasons for listening.[2] Along the way we have discovered how difficult it is to connect the two; for example, Denisoff and Levine discovered that college students had little accurate understanding of a popular social protest hit they were all familiar with;[3] Robinson and Hirsch demonstrated that in some cases it was hard enough for the researchers themselves to correctly interpret song content.[4] Moreover, the reliability of this research has been continually challenged by the enormity of the undertaking—understanding the intricacy and complexity of the relationship between an individual and the pervasive, ubiquitous, diverse culture that surrounds him.

We still need a coherent paradigm for the interaction of popular music and its audience, one which provides a significant starting point for further research as well as a framework for a more accurate and more reliable model. This chapter attempts to outline such a paradigm of the dynamics of popular music.

We can render the dynamics of popular music visually by portraying it as a complex of interacting parts, perhaps best envisioned as smaller triads within one master triad (Figure 5). The dynamics are composed of three elements: composition, performance, and response. Each of these is influenced by the other two: composition by the intention of performance and the expectation of response; performance by the nature of the composition and the expectation of response; response by the nature of the composition and the execution of performance. Music is an act of communication and, as such, is necessarily composed of these inseparable elements, although these elements may not always be of equal importance. Moreover, each of these elements is itself composed of inseparable interacting elements.

Composition includes lyrics, melody, and arrangement, each one variable in response to the others. Lyrics are shaped to fit melody, melody is made to contain lyrics, arrangements are designed to express both words and music. In popular songs, these variables can often be disproportionate and any one of them can dominate. For example, songwriters like Harry Chapin and Bob Dylan emphasize words over music, while Phil Spector and Neil Diamond emphasize arrangement and Paul McCartney very often emphasizes melody. This is not to suggest that they ignore the other elements, merely that they allow one element to predominate. Of these three elements, arrangement is most directly tied to performance, since it is principally a means of preparing for it.

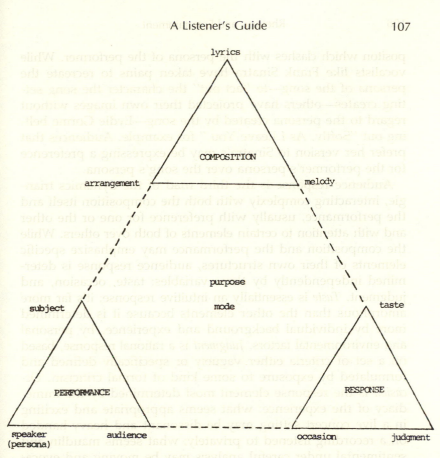

**Figure 5.**
**The Dynamics of Popular Music**

Performance is really a variation of the communication triangle, made up of speaker, subject, and audience, with their
corresponding appeals to ethos, logos, and pathos. In performance of popular music we have a singer singing about something to a listener or listeners, and the emphasis of that experience can be on any one of these three elements, although
never exclusively so. We should also point out that the persona
of the singer and the persona of the character telling the story
or reciting the ideas and emotions of the song may be confused
in performance. A songwriter may create a persona in the com-

positon which clashes with the persona of the performer. While vocalists like Frank Sinatra have taken pains to recreate the persona of the song—to "act out" the character the song setting creates—others have projected their own images without regard to the persona created by the song—Eydie Gorme belting out "Softly, As I Leave You," for example. Audiences that prefer her version to Sinatra's may be expressing a preference for the performer's persona over the song's persona.

Audience response is the third triad of the dynamics triangle, interacting complexly with both the composition itself and the performance, usually with preference for one or the other and with attention to certain elements of both over others. While the composition and the performance may emphasize specific elements of their own structures, audience response is determined independently by three variables: taste, occasion, and judgment. *Taste* is essentially an intuitive response; it's far more amorphous than the other elements because it is determined more by individual background and experience, by personal and environmental factors. *Judgment* is a rational response, based on a set of criteria either vaguely or specifically defined and formulated by exposure to some kind of formal criticism. *Occasion* is the response element most determined by the immediacy of the experience; what seems appropriate and exciting in a live concert setting may be dissonant and heavy-handed on a recording listened to privately; what seems maudlin and sentimental under careful analysis may be moving and evocative in a private, intimate moment. As with composition and performance, the elements of the response triad are highly interactive and inseparable, although one may take precedence over the others in specific circumstances.

Impinging on the overall interaction of composition, performance, and response are two additional factors: purpose and mode. *Purpose* entails the reason for composition and performance, the effect or the goal that the songwriter and/or the performer hope to achieve. *Mode* has to do with the form of the composition or performance as regards established, identifiable kinds of music, for example bluegrass, blues, disco. Purpose is an important factor of all rhetorical situations since a good deal of communication success is measured by how well it achieves its purpose; mode is equally important because it places limitations on composition and performance beyond which they cannot go without becoming quite another kind of composition or performance altogether.

It is quite important to recognize the nature of the dynamics of popular music before examining more closely its rhetorical elements in order to avoid the simplistic categorizations that the following discussion might invite. In this context we are more aware of the complexities of interaction which underlie the rhetorical elements of popular song which will be isolated and examined in the following pages.

In analyzing the rhetoric of popular song, it is important to remember that it is both the means for communication by the artist and the system of response by the audience, and that its elements interact in complex ways. Some hint of the complexity of response lies in John Lahr's reminiscences about early rock 'n' roll and the fantasy life the music evoked for him:

Virgin, I lived in the dream of rock's sexual promise. . . . My fantasy at these rock shows (they weren't "concerts" until later) was this: I'd put my arm around one of those vixens with pointed tits. A hood would bop over and ask if I wanted a mouthful of bloody chicklets. "My hands are registered," I'd say. He'd walk away. The girl would lay her painted lips on mine as Frankie Lymon sang, "Why do fools fall in love?"[5]

Some part of the way audiences respond to music has to do with the fantasies it helps them create, its effect on their moods. In a study of "Gratifications and Expectations Associated with Pop Music Among Adolescents," a research team discovered that 79 percent of the high school and college students responding claimed that pop music frequently "gets me in or keeps me in a mood I want to be in."[6] As Lahr puts it, "the music went everywhere with me. Chuck Berry for waking up, the Shirelles for whacking off, the Coasters for a late night laugh." He emphasizes the ubiquitousness of the music: "Humping in the back of cars, studying in bed before lights-out, cruising the city in a friend's set of wheels—we were all sealed in a wall of sound which was the backdrop of every personal event."[7] In such a statement we can recognize the variety of personal response inherent in the listening attitudes of pop song audiences.

Part of the fantasy life inspired by pop music is related to identification with the speaker, that is, with either the persona created by the singer and/or composer or the persona projected by the singer regardless of the song. Bob Reiss describes this instance of a fan's fantasy identification with Linda Ronstadt:

Liz has never met Linda but nevertheless considers her a comrade in interpersonal hardships. After all, Ronstadt is always singing those heart-break ballads, especially "Long, Long Time," and Liz used to have this boyfriend who . . . well . . . got transferred away to California.

When Liz is depressed about the boyfriend, she goes into an alcove in her parents' Bethesda home, dons stereo headphones, and that woeful Ronstadt voice envelopes her, the smoky rambling ballads, the gutsy blues. *Linda feels the same way I do*, she thinks, and suddenly evokes on her inner eyelids not a picture of Linda Ronstadt but of herself, the flower in her hair, pouring out her own feelings so that thousands feel shivers running up and down their spines. Lovers hold each other. Strangers gape. Scattered in the audience, melancholy looks on their faces, are all her old boyfriends, shaking their heads and thinking, Look what I missed. I should have stuck around.[8]

Identification with the speaker can alter a preference for two similar songs. For example, both "Tonight's the Night," written and performed by Rod Stewart, and "We've Got Tonite," written and performed by Bob Seger, are essentially seduction songs; each centers on a situation in which a man is trying to talk a woman into bed. The chief difference lies in the presentation of the speaker's persona.

In "Tonight's the Night" the man is instructing a younger woman, not only initiating her into sex but also ordering her preparation for it:

> Stay away from my window
> Stay away from my back door too
> Disconnect the telephone line
> Relax, baby, and draw that blind

The emphasis is on the man's expectations:

> Come on, angel, my heart's on fire
> Don't deny your man's desire
> You'd be a fool to stop this tide
> Spread your wings and let me come inside

The melody and arrangement reinforce a seductive rhythm running through the song and the lyrics paint a picture of the man's anticipation and control of the situation:

> 'Cause tonight's the night
> It's gonna be alright
> 'Cause I love you, girl
> Ain't nobody gonna stop us now.[9]

On the other hand, "We've Got Tonite" offers a speaker who understands the woman's position and expresses a sense of their mutual needs:

> I know it's late. I know you're weary
> I know your plans don't include me
> Still here we are, both of us lonely
> Longing for shelter from all that we see

He attempts to use persuasion, trying to convince rather than control:

> Why should we worry? No one will care, girl
> Look at the stars, so far away
> We've got tonight. Who needs tomorrow?
> We've got tonight. Why don't you stay?

He expresses his own situation frankly and offers the woman the opportunity to make the decision:

> Deep in my soul I've been so lonely
> All of my hopes fading away
> I've longed for love, like everyone else does
> I know I'll keep searching, even after today
> So there it is, girl, I've said it all now,
> And here we are, what do you say?[10]

The song concludes with the repetition of earlier lines and the chorus, heightened in intensity by the arrangement.

While a great deal more might be said about each song, the distinction between personae is clear, and preference for the song may vary with the listener's ability to identify with the speaker. If the sense of emphasis on the speaker were not so strong, we might well be more concerned with the way the songs handle their common subject. What sometimes draws us to a song is its approach to its theme or topic. For example, during the 1970's, popular hits included a number of sexual initiation songs, including "December 1965 (Oh What a Night!)," recorded by Frankie Valli, "Summer, The First Time," recorded by Bobby Goldsboro, "Desiree," by Neil Diamond, and "Night Moves," by Bob Seger. While the personae of these songs are not identical, they are chiefly differentiated by the perspective they provide for the subject. For example, "Desiree" is essentially a celebration of sexual initiation which equates the narrator's youthful introduction to sex by an older woman with achieving manhood.[11] It presents the situation from the point of view of a young male triumphantly losing his virginity and uses metaphor and melody to romanticize the experience. On the other hand, Seger's "Night Moves," a richly rewarding song on a number of levels, candidly presents the young lovers as mutual explorers of sexual experience:

> We weren't in love, O, no, far from it
> We weren't searching for some pie-in-the-sky summit
> We were just young and restless and bored
> living by the sword
> And we'd steal away every chance we could
> to the backroom, the alley, or the trusty woods
> I used her, she used me
> But neither one cared
> We were getting our share.[12]

Unlike "Desiree" and other period songs, "Night Moves" is not romantic nostalgia; rather it is a reflective reminiscence which ties the energetic portion describing youthful sex to a more contemplative epilogue placing the speaker in maturer circumstances. The sexual encounter section moves to the following crescendo:

> Workin' on those night moves
> Tryin' to lose those awkward teenage blues
> Working on the night moves
> and it was summertime
> And, oh, the wonder
> Felt the lightnin' and we waited on the thunder
> Waited on the thunder

The music shifts pace and instrumentation to present a slower, sparer section:

> I woke last night to the sound of thunder
> How far off I sat and wondered
> Started hummin' a song from 1962
> Ain't it funny how the night moves
> When you just don't seem to have as much to lose
> Strange how the night moves
> With autumn closing in.

The song ends with a return to the music of the earlier section.

In this analysis it is evident that the treatment of the theme of sexual initiation in "Night Moves" has been carried out from a different perspective, with different insights and emotions, than in "Desiree." The approach to the subject may vary the listener's preference for the song.

As in any rhetorical situation, consideration for the audience may influence or decide the ways in which the speaker is presented and the subject is handled: lyrically, anyway, Seger's "Night Moves" is directed at a mature audience, one which can accept the persona of an older man and perhaps identify with it, and one which can accept its unromantic view of sexual initiation and the passivity that comes with maturity. But audience can also serve as a major factor in composition and response. For example, Paul McCartney's "Let It Be" stays the same both in the area of persona of the speaker of the song (if not the persona of the performer) and also in the area of subject treatment regardless of who records it. But the arrangement may alter considerably to provide for audience expectations. The Beatles' own version is rock oriented; Joan Baez's version is folk oriented; Aretha Franklin's is soul oriented. Audience considerations figure in the arrangements of songs covered by performers other than the original composers; they may also suggest a change in the tastes of audiences over the years. For example, compare Joan Baez's folk version of "House of the Rising Sun" with the blues-rock version by the Animals, the psychedelic version by Frigid Pink, and the recent country-disco version by Dolly Parton. That attention to the rhetorical element of audience must be a consideration during production of a record and response to a performance is borne out by the findings of Robinson and Hirsch that "the stratified teenage audience (usually viewed by adults as an undifferentiated horde) is an aggregate of individuals who form distinct popular music subaudiences . . . with little crossover in membership."[13]

Speaker, subject, and audience are interactive elements of a rhetorical or communication situation; less distinct and more pervasive an element is purpose. A composition is usually created to effect some aim or end or goal. If the purpose is to stir an audience to a pitch of patriotism or martial fervor, the rhetorical elements must be adapted in special ways; if the purpose is to provide an occasion for dancing, different adaptations must be made; if the purpose is to provide a background for romance, still different adaptations must occur. Purpose lies behind the differences among "The Stars and Stripes Forever," "Stars on 45," and "Stars Fell on Alabama."

Clearer examples are provided by looking at three songs written and performed by the Bee Gees in the film *Saturday Night Fever*. The movie opens with the song "Stayin' Alive," played while the hero, Tony, struts down a Brooklyn street, moving to the rhythm of the song, while everyone else either plods or walks. The song's lyrics identify for us his outlook on life, his sense of isolation, his withdrawal from meaningful involvement:

> You can tell by the way I use my walk
> I'm a woman's man, no time to talk
> Music loud and woman warm

I've been kicked around since I was born
But it's allright, it's okay
I'll live to see another day.[14]

The character is simply "stayin' alive, stayin' alive." Midway in the film the song "Night Fever" is played, first as part of a fantasy as Tony dresses at home, then as part of Tony's night at the disco; in both cases the song helps illustrate the release, the escape, that he finds in dancing. By the end of the film his position of defensive isolation has become untenable and his satisfaction in dancing dissipates; he turns toward the one character who can help him understand his life and possibly find direction for it, Stephanie. The film closes on Tony's cross-city journey to Stephanie, accompanied by "How Deep Is Your Love?," a song principally about needing and believing in another person:

How deep is your love? How deep is your love?
I really mean to learn
'Cause we're living in a world of fools breaking us down
When they all should let us be
We belong to you and me
I believe in you
You know the door to my very soul
You're the light in my deepest, darkest hour
You're my saviour when I fall.[15]

The songs illuminate the context in which they are played; to respond to them simply as disco numbers is to miss their purpose.

But, of course, they are disco numbers, and while the mode of presentation is not as vital here as elsewhere, in fact mode can be a principal determinant of response, as well as of composition. Disco is a kind of music, demanding by definition specific kinds of effects; so are the blues; so is bluegrass; so is rockabilly. At times the composer may simply be trying to write a song in a certain mode or choosing a certain mode for an expected result. In any case the mode limits the response to the song just as it limits the possibilities for composition: you can only go so far within a specifically defined genre of music before you have abandoned it. A curious feature of much music currently classified as "country" is that it uses none of the instrumentation or arrangements commonly associated with country music; for example, Barbara Mandrell's song, "I Was Country When Country Wasn't Cool," is far more a middle-of-the-road pop tune than a country song. Further illustration of this point may be found by comparing two songs recorded on the same album by Nicolette Larson, one a bouncy dance tune by Jesse Winchester called "Rhumba Girl" and the other a bluegrass ballad by Charlie and Ira Louvin called "Angels Rejoiced." Both songs are arranged in a certain mode—to do otherwise would violate their initial premises; in following generic arrangements Larson eliminates any strong sense of her own identity as a performer.[16]

For the most part, the discussion of the rhetorical elements of popular music has focused on the lyrics of the songs presented, but melody and arrangement are also contributors to the rhetoric of popular song, helping to establish a persona for the singer, clarify the impression of the subject, and meet the needs of the audience; they also serve the purposes of both composition and performance and by and large they define mode, regardless of the lyrics.

The paradigm offered on the preceding pages is by no means the only possible model for the dynamics of popular music, but it does highlight the essential elements in a way that allows for extended analysis of the composition, the performance, and the audience response. As such it ought to be a useful tool for researchers attempting to respond to the complexity of popular music's effect upon its audience, and it ought to help that audience differentiate among the kinds of responses it makes. Of course, we can't completely confine our responses to one rhetorical element or limit them to one kind of response. If the music is complex, the intellect, emotion, and experience of the listener is even more complex. When song and listener interact, the result may defy our best efforts at analysis.

# 10

# A Viewer's Guide to the Rhetoric of Television

The dynamics of television drama include dimensions of program composition, program reception, and discourse. We may picture the dynamics of television in the same way we pictured the dynamics of popular music in the previous chapter, as three interacting triangles dealing with composition, rhetoric, and audience. That is, we can keep the triangle of viewer reaction or response (taste, occasion and judgment) and the triangle of rhetoric or performance (ethos, pathos, logos) and change the terms in the triangle of composition from lyrics, melody, and arrangement to language, images, and sound, the interactive components of every television program (Figure 6). While composition and response are significant aspects of this dynamic, this chapter will attend chiefly to the rhetorical aspect of television.

There are several ways of talking about the rhetoric of television, and all of them, to some degree, involve re-defining the special features of rhetoric in terms of the special features of the television medium. Joel Nydahl, in attempting to define a "rhetoric of network news," demonstrates a means of converting or elaborating upon rhetorical features:

in any definition of *rhetoric* that pretends to encompass television, terms usually associated with print or oratory would have to take on expanded meaning: *content* and *style*, for example, would have to be

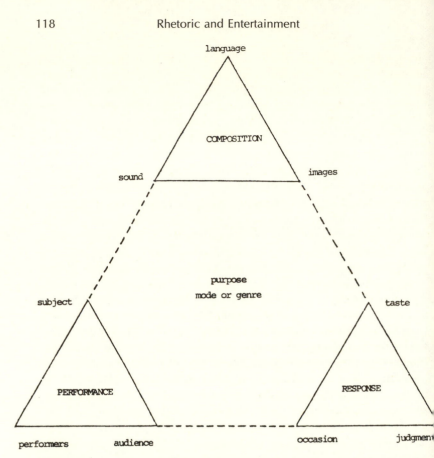

**Figure 6.**
**The Dynamics of Television Drama**

thought of as containing such televisual elements as shot selection and camera angles; *structure* as encompassing everything from the arrangement of shots (montage) to the placement of stories within news programs or even news programs within a daily schedule; *cadence* as meaning not only the pattern and pace of shots but also the interplay among visual, verbal, and auditory elements; *oratory* as including all manner of oral, auditory, and imagistic presentations; and *language* as subsuming all verbal, visual, and auditory structures of meaning.[1]

In another approach, Ronald Primeau applies the five parts of rhetoric—invention, arrangement, style, delivery, and memory—to the production of television programs:

invention as the process of creativity from initial brainstorms to an audition and the making of a television "pilot"; arrangement, from the classical *dispositio* to modern form; style, from the personal flair of self-expression to making a celebrity in our "star" system; production techniques in TV, from a shooting script to a finished product; and methods used to store and retrieve material in order to make it memorable.[2]

Both of these methods seem to me useful and productive; nevertheless, I want to focus attention on a third way of applying rhetorical analysis to television, the one we have been using so far in this book, by examining the ethos, pathos, logos, purpose, and mode of individual television programs. When we understand how these elements act upon the television program and also upon the viewer, we have a reliable means by which we may analyze a show or series for its rhetorical effect. Every television program has a point of view, a perspective, whether implied or explicit; it has a worldview which is promulgated by elements essential to its composition and both aesthetic and rhetorical at the same time.

Just as we can talk about ethos in regard to a person or speaker, we can also talk about the ethos of a television program or series. Each television series has an ethos of its own, a sense of character about the entire program, not only about the individual characters which populate the program. Each character also projects an ethos, of course, and it is the combination of those personalities together with other aspects of the program that make up the ethos of the series. One way to see the ethos of a television series at work is to examine the weekly opening credits, which are a condensed representation of the series, attempting to establish the kind of show it is and the kind of expectations viewers should have for typical episodes.

For example, the comedy series *Kate and Allie* has a standard opening sequence. At the start of the program the theme music comes up for just a few seconds while the camera establishes a general locale, usually a New York exterior, and then the music fades and the two principal characters, Kate (played by Susan St. James) and Allie (played by Jane Curtin) come into view in the midst of a conversation. Usually the two sit or stroll together chatting casually about some mundane topic—refusing to buy eyeglasses, going to cocktail parties, an acquaintance getting divorced, growing older. The segment is usually mildly amusing but never particularly relevant to the evening's episode; they are less previews of the show to follow than vignettes establishing the relationship between the two women. Although occasionally they express conflicting viewpoints characteristic of their personalities in the series, they are primarily identified as simply two relaxed, intimate women "being themselves," open, revealing, and vulnerable with one another.

The opening credits which follow this introductory segment serve to establish the identity of the two stars and the general personae of their characters. The montage of poses and activities chiefly identifies them as talkers who interrelate mostly with one another. If we compare the opening of *Kate and Allie* with those of two other comedy series ostensibly about single parents, *Alice* and *One Day at a Time*, we find the emphasis on intimate talk unique to only one of them. *Alice* is not principally about single-parenting or adjusting to living alone after marriage, in spite of a title song which talks about getting rid of blinders and getting out and looking for oneself. The images of the credits are chiefly on slapstick events in the diner where Alice works, not on her relationship with her son or neighbors, and the chief characters are co-workers, not family. *One Day at a Time* emphasizes individual characters in the credits and an extended family which includes the apartment building superintendent, but the action of the montage is generally highly energetic and the sense of movement and pace is very brisk and dynamic. In fact this series is far more aggressive and far more dependent on confrontation than *Kate and Allie* and reveals its different ethos in its credits.

Each episode of *Kate and Allie* reinforces the intimations of the opening credits. The women are divorcees and single parents. Kate is peppy, flippant, sexually adventurous, experienced; she has one child, a daughter named Emma, and an exhusband, Max, who is an actor and a generally charming, adventurous, but unreliable person. Allie is straight, uptight, demure, inexperienced, the woman who married her ideal man, served him as a dedicated keeper of his home and nurturer for his children, lived a stereotypical suburban life as a doctor's wife, and lost him to a younger, more glamorous woman; she has two children, a teen-aged daughter, Jenny, and a younger son, Chip, and an ex-husband named Charles whose second wife is named Clare.

The balance between their roles allows a wide-ranging ethos— between them the two women are apt to represent and/or encounter the full range of marital, parental, and divorce experiences. But the sense of intimacy in the opening segment and the establishment in the credits of a joint single-parent household create the sense of these characters as candid, loving, amusing, and thoughtful, and focuses the viewer's attention on those aspects of the show. The ethical appeal established in the opening portion of the program and adhered to throughout each episode is the identity of the series, the program persona to which the viewer reacts.

To further demonstrate the ways in which the ethos of a series is defined in the opening credits, consider two rather different dramatic series on CBS: *Cagney and Lacey* and *Scarecrow and Mrs. King*.

The opening credits of *Cagney and Lacey* feature the standard montage revolving around the central characters. Bouncy music in the background underscores their constant movement, beginning with a shot of them walking down the street together, side by side, talking. The subsequent series of images divides its attention between the two women and occasionally gives them equal space on screen or parallel time. We see them talking, laughing, speaking on the phone, working with others, bustling about police headquarters. The other cast members who are introduced are also shown in the work environment, usually in both serious and relaxed poses. The attention on the title characters switches to an emphasis on the dangerous side of their profession only toward the end of the credits, when we see them running down the street, running through a subway, racing up and down stairs, pointing their service revolvers and mouthing commands, and escorting an arrest past a flasher. In the final shot Mary Beth Lacey (Tyne Daly) in a bowling shirt and Christine Cagney (Sharon Gless) in a fur coat are prevented from leaving their office by their lieutenant who points them in the opposite direction, and the freeze frame on their annoyed, dismayed expressions leaves us with the impression of them as overworked cops.

The opening credits establish this show as a series about the relationship between two women as co-workers and as police officers, emphasizing their friendship, their constant interaction, their roles as friends, workers, and individuals. Each episode further enlarges upon these elements, by balancing Mary Beth's professional responsibilities with her obligations to her husband and children and Chris' dedication to her career with her difficulties as a single working woman, and by continually emphasizing conflicts between the two women and between them and their work environment. The identity of the show revolves around our sense of Cagney and Lacey as friends, as working women, and police officers, in that order.

As with the two series we've just been examining, the opening credits of *Scarecrow and Mrs. King* also use visual and musical cues to create a sense of identity. In a brief montage Kate Jackson, as Amanda King, is shown in domestic scenes—dressing children, vacuuming around the children at play, counting shoes in her closet—and the music is light, bouncy, busy; both visuals and theme music establish Amanda as a homemaker and mother, a woman somewhat harried but still lighthearted. When the credits turn their attention to her co-star, Bruce Boxleitner as Lee Stetson (code name, Scarecrow), both the visuals and the theme music change. The music becomes heavier, more lush, more exciting, and the visuals show Scarecrow as both hero and spy—exploring dark rooms with gun or flashlight in hand, rolling on the ground as if avoiding gunfire, running as if in pursuit. The two characters are shown together for the first time under this exciting theme music, and then the supporting cast is introduced, including Amanda's mother and children and Scarecrow's chief and Agency colleague. The visuals then highlight the action side of the series and the interaction of the two principals, ending on a light-hearted scene of Amanda in the street with Scarecrow disguised as a cabdriver.

The credits blend both situation-comedy situations and action-adventure situations and identify the show's basic premise—a Washington widowed single parent becomes the teammate of an experienced, daring spy. Amanda King is always earnest, sincere, bright, but somewhat flighty, naive, and ingenuous. Her concern for her mother and her children, her continual reversion to a middle-class domestic frame of reference, identify her as chiefly comic (although never ridiculous). Scarecrow, on the other hand, is stalwart, serious, competent, knowledgeable, and bold. His frame of reference is always the Agency or the espionage business. Her instincts as an average woman always clash with his instincts as a professional spy, and he continually gains a grudging acceptance and even affection for her. Often the show suggests that the two are only an episode away from having a love relationship except for the necessity of staying emotionally uninvolved in their work.

While no program is required to follow through on their opening credits or to guarantee that they are entirely representative of the episode to follow, usually the ethos established at the beginning of the program is consistent with that portrayed in the episode, if only because the montage is taken from one or more episodes of the series. The establishment of an easily identifiable ethos is important to a program because it is one of the chief appeals to an audience—a series where the ethos is difficult to define, or at least to intuit, loses a significant means of attracting viewers.

In television, the pathos of a program lies in its attempts to amuse or excite the viewer, to involve him in the action of the program or the lives of the characters. To some degree television series depend upon the viewers' involvement with the characters, the frequent exposure to them which creates certain predictability about their behavior. The quick establishment of ethos in the opening credits is a way of creating that involvement, but the ensuing interest in the characters and in the situations of the series has to depend on viewer interest. The question is seldom, "What theme will the show explore this week?" or "What question will the series tackle in the next episode?" but rather "What variations on this formula that I enjoy so much will the show work this week?" or "What will happen to the chief characters and how will it affect their development as characters?"

In *Kate and Allie* the pathetic appeal centers on interest in the problems of being divorced, being single parents, and being two women as heads of a household. Individual episodes revolve around attraction to an ex-marriage partner, competition for children's attention, presumption of sexual orientation because of the living arrangement, coping with grief over divorce, and similar complications normally related to the situation of the title characters. The pathos is directed at an audience willing to accept these subjects as the fit topics of situational drama and willing to have them treated with a combination of wit and sentimentality. The two women are flip and verbal, but the comic dialogue is usually consistent with the characters and occasionally causes conflict between them. The dialogue advances the fears and concerns of the characters about the situations in which they find themselves, and the problems usually have to be dealt with in at least a semi-serious manner. If the show should shift its appeal to the audience's emotions by opting for the pat, sentimental conclusions of other situation comedy series, or by adopting a stridently feminist position, the kind of viewer it appeals to would change, and indeed the kind of viewer it already has probably comes to it because of a certain amount of compatibility he or she shares with the program about its treatment of its principal situation.

*Scarecrow and Mrs. King* balances its pathetic appeal between thrills and laughter. Comic moments highlighting Amanda's ineptitude or naiveté and Lee's frustration alternate with action moments in which Amanda is threatened or chased or Lee is fighting or pursuing villains. The appeal to the audience is to both their sense of adventure and their sense of amusement; identification with the characters aids viewer involvement, of course, but there is additional concern that Amanda will have to reveal her dual life to her mother or that her agency involvement will endanger her family. Routinely, it endangers her, and the excitement of that endangerment is enhanced by the sense that Amanda is not a trained spy but, rather, an average person. The audience for the program has to be willing to take espionage lightly, to enjoy the contrast between genres in the series, the placement of a situation comedy character in adventure circumstances, the difficulty of an adventure character coping with a situation comedy context.

In *Cagney and Lacey*, as well, the pathetic appeal is mixed, between a concern for these characters' domestic lives—the problem of mixing family and career, the tension of divided loyalties, the conflicts of working closely with another person—and a concern for these characters' professional lives—the interest in police procedures, the excitement over the danger and adventure of detective work. The particular identity of the show as a series about working women also adds unique concerns in the dangers to the characters as women in traditionally male-oriented roles, as well as the conflicts of moral and social dilemmas.

Each series, no matter what its similarity to other series in format or genre, establishes individual characteristics which alter the ways audiences respond to it. Just as the ethos and the pathos of each series is unique, so is its characteristic logos. In television drama, the logos is the presentation of actions and ideas during the course of the program which persuade us to adopt the point of view of the show. An individual episode has its own logos, its own presentation of evidence, and through the establishment of the logos of individual episodes, a series, if it has any consistency at all, will evolve a cumulative logos of its own.

For example, one episode of *Magnum, P. I.* revolves around Magnum's being lost alone at sea without supplies of any kind and ends with his discovery by friends who, in the whole of the Pacific Ocean, look in the correct location guided by instinct, intuition, and emotional commitment. In another episode one of Magnum's friends is critically injured in a helicopter crash and someone claiming to be his brother shows up to keep a bedside vigil. At one point the attending physician indicates that he has done all he can and that the man's only hope is that the closeness of those who love him will assist his own will to live to bring him out of his coma. Only when the brother is absent and one of the series' continuing characters sits by the patient does he revive, thus revealing to Magnum that the brother is a phony—a real brother's presence would have penetrated the coma. These two episodes reveal an implied metaphysics unique to this series, a persistent worldview about the mystical nature of male bonding. Our choice is to accept or reject the logos of this worldview in the individual episode or in the series at large.

In terms of *Kate and Allie* the logos of the series usually revolves around working through a problem related to divorce and/or single parenting. In one episode, which begins with Kate's ex-husband, Max, moving to LA in hopes of an acting career, it is made clear that Kate has encouraged him and that their daughter Emma is heartbroken by the loss of her father. When Emma begins taking piano lessons from a young singer-songwriter named Walter and develops a crush on him, Kate first credits the lessons for the revival of Emma's spirits—she's been given her father's piano—and then learns that the infatuation with Walter is the key. The mid-show commercial begins with that revelation and the second half of the show deals with Walter's attraction to Kate and Emma's resentment of it which leads to the discovery that Emma blames Kate for her father's move to California and has been looking for male reinforcement. Mother and daughter make up, talk out their problems, and understand one another better by the end of the episode. The development of the drama in the episode is keyed to relevant issues about the loss of a parent, the need for certain kinds of reinforcement, and the problem of certain kinds of rivalry. The success of the show depends upon the viewer's acceptance of the argument of the program.

In another episode Allie resents her ex-husband's lavish gifts of a personal computer and extravagant entertainment for their son, Chip, and counters with a full-grown dog that wreaks havoc on the household, leading her to consider giving the dog away. In the course of dealing with her son's resentment, Allie expresses her anger to Charles who counters with an explanation of his extravagance as an attempt to make the little time he has with his son special. The happy ending of the episode comes in the father's offer to keep the dog at his place in the country, the agreement of both parents to discuss gifts and expenses for the children, and the mother's realization that the father's extravagant gift of the home computer will be staying in *her* home.

The two episodes outlined above reveal the logos of the series—the belief that people can solve their problems by examining them, admitting them, and talking them out, coupled with candor about the fallibility of the main characters and their admirable attempts to do better. Unlike some programs which allow twenty-five minutes of comically reinforced anti-social behavior to precede five minutes of repentance and elaborate sentimentality, the emphasis on commonplaces of real-life situations logically modeled gives this series a distinctive approach to its "argument."

In addition to the three kinds of appeal it must have, each discourse also has a *purpose* or aim influencing the nature of the appeals made. While it is always hard to define a show's purpose in terms of its presentation without falling prey to the intentional fallacy (the belief that a viewer can recognize what the show's producers "intend" to achieve), the consistent representation of certain characters, certain appeals to the audience, certain habits of presentation—in other words, a series' ethos, pathos, and logos—can make it possible to generalize about purpose.

For example, in *Kate and Allie* the emphasis on verbal humor and situations growing specifically out of circumstances related to the leading characters' marital states and domestic living arrangements as well as the de-emphasis on certain conventions of situation comedy such as rapid-fire one-liners, farcical misunderstandings, and stock characters suggest that the purpose of the series is to explore in comic but realistic terms the particular circumstances of divorced women and single-parents in a way which attempts to address their problems and either resolve them or model behaviors relating to them in believable and psychologically valid ways without excessive sentimentality, derogatory characterizations, or sociologically undesirable behaviors. This is not to suggest any superiority of these purposes to those of shows with somewhat similar formats—the early episodes of *One Day at a Time*, for example, or other shows with single parents like *Different Strokes*, *Silver Spoons*, or *Gimme a Break*. It does suggest distinctions which help identify the particular nature of such programs, however.

If we consider the purpose of *Kate and Allie* to be the one I have suggested, then certain things have to happen in the series and certain things cannot or should not occur. The kinds of characters who appear, the kinds of situations which occur, the kinds of resolutions of problems and interactions of characters which take place all need to be consistent with its purpose. In seeking that consistency, the particular ethos, pathos, and logos of the series will be generated.

To give a sense of how purpose can help define differences between shows, we need only look at two programs with a similar format, *Scarecrow and Mrs. King* and *Cover-up*. Both are about female amateurs teaming up with male professionals in the espionage arena. But *Scarecrow and Mrs. King* intends to provide more light-hearted entertainment than *Cover Up* does. We can see that by comparing the ethos of the second show with that of the one we've examined already. In *Cover Up*'s credits the alternation between woman and man is between a sophisticated, elegant fashion photographer accustomed to posh surroundings and a rugged, resourceful man used to survival through guerrilla tactics under grueling circumstances—she's shown in a luxurious restaurant, he's shown eating out of a can with a knife in a jungle setting. The woman is far more competent, sophisticated, and daring than Amanda King, the man more violent, more experienced in commando tactics, more of a killer than Scarecrow. The difference in ethos makes clear the difference in purpose—*Cover Up* intends to provide more intense, more adult adventure than *Scarecrow and Mrs. King* offers in a similar format.

The final element necessary for rhetorical analysis of a television show is *mode* or genre, the kind of program that it is. Certain expectations are created, certain conventions need to be followed, if the program is a series, a mini-series, or a television motion picture, and whether it is a situation comedy, a police drama, a mystery, an action-adventure series, an espionage drama. Working within conventional modes gives producers and directors easy shorthand by which to communicate with audiences; it also limits them in the possibilities of character and situation, unless they are particularly innovative and daring.

The mode of *Kate and Allie* is situation comedy and the impact of the mode upon the program affects the conduct of the characters and the kind of resolutions that they can reach concerning their problems. All television series demand that the action revolve around the chief characters, that the chief characters survive the episode, and that the episode be complete in itself with little continuing effect on the conduct of the series. Viewers accept these conventions and only critics complain if a husband's near-affair on a situation comedy one week has no repercussions in the marriage the next week, or if the action hero's injuries at the end of one week's adventures are completely healed and forgotten by the following week. Conventions of drama in every mode make certain demands upon the ways the elements are generated and performed and upon the viewer's reaction to them.

In a situation comedy the humor is very important, obviously; in a domestic drama the attention to real-life crises is important. As a situation comedy series, *Kate and Allie* does not attempt much carry-over from week-to-week, develops no serial plotlines, and focuses on more mundane matters than life and death situations or tragic circumstances. In addition to asking what mode a program is in, we also need to consider how well it functions within the conventions of the mode.

In applying the five elements of rhetorical analysis to television programming, I have been obliged to present them linearly and separately, but of course their interaction with one another and their impact on the program itself are simultaneous and complementary. Mode affects logos, purpose affects pathos, and all influence and are influenced by ethos. Nonetheless, an attempt to identify these elements separately provides a rhetorical analysis which helps explain not only the ways in which a television series attracts viewers but also the ways in which it influences them.

As I pointed out earlier, viewer response is typically predicated upon taste, occasion, or judgment. The television program may not so much create the taste as satisfy it—the viewer looks for certain kinds of programming based on past experience and personal preference. The choice that a viewer makes between *Knight Rider* and *Murder, She Wrote*—that is, between an action show about a man's relationship with a computer-driven car and a mystery show about a genteel writer-detective—both telecast at the same time, may have less to do with a sense of each program's quality than with the viewer's age and sex. On the other hand, a fan of detective shows would probably use judgment to distinguish between *Matt Houston* and

*Mickey Spillane's Mike Hammer*—his preference for the show would depend upon his view of what qualities such a show ought to have. In the matter of occasion, the viewer's choices depend upon whether he's watching alone, with his wife, or with his family, whether he's had a hard day at work or home, what kind of social issues he feels obliged to keep conversant with, and so on.

The rhetoric of television makes the appeals upon which the viewer selects the program; in this regard, the viewer is independent, and the rhetorical elements do more to define the viewership than to determine it. But those same arguments argue for the point of view that the program establishes, deliberately or inadvertently, and it is this aspect that a rhetorical analysis can make clear.

George Orwell once wrote:

> every writer, especially every novelist, *has* a "message," whether he admits it or not, and the minutest details of his work are influenced by it. All art is propaganda.[3]

The statement seems to me to be as true of popular culture as of literature, particularly in television, film, and popular music, which are at base simply forms of literary media. Orwell's observation is akin to Horace Newcomb's assertion that "television is a crucially important object of study . . . because it brings its massive audience into a direct relationship with particular sets of values and attitudes."[4] Even in such a cooperative, collective enterprise, some assumptions about the ways the world works or ought to work underlie the creative process, and the resultant product will serve as an endorsement of that worldview regardless of its creators' intentions. A rhetorical analysis does not help determine the aesthetic qualities of various works, although it may help explain some viewer's preferences for one show over another; but it does help to determine the message, implicit or explicit, which is the cumulative effect of the program or series, and thus offers the viewer some options about the kind of worldview he decides to endorse by watching or to promote by allowing his children to watch.

# 11

# A Reader's Guide to the Rhetoric of Popular Fiction

In the preface to *The Rhetoric of Fiction*, Wayne C. Booth expressed his sense of the applicability of rhetorical analysis to non-persuasive fiction:

In writing about the rhetoric of fiction, I am not primarily interested in didactic fiction, fiction used for propaganda or instruction. My subject is the technique of non-didactic fiction, viewed as the art of communicating with readers—the rhetorical resources available to the writer of epic, novel, or short story as he tries, consciously or unconsciously, to impose his fictional world upon the reader.[1]

His argument here reinforces a central argument of this book—the validity of rhetorical analysis to the study of all communication or discourse, not solely argumentative or oratorical discourse. Booth's use of the term "impose his fictional world upon the reader" echoes that of George Orwell some twenty years earlier, that "every artist is a propagandist in the sense that he is trying, directly or indirectly, to impose a vision of life that seems to him desirable."[2] Both Orwell and Booth agree that a writer has a world view that is represented in his work, whether the work is expressly polemical and didactic or explicitly non-political and non-didactic in intention. The worldview is there in the writer before he begins writing, and the kind of world he creates in prose will reflect it and "impose" itself upon the reader. This is not to say that the reader necessarily either disagrees with the worldview or accepts it—the reader's response to a literary work is as much ruled by taste, occasion, and judgment as is his response to any other art form—but it does suggest that an understanding of the literary work through rhetorical analysis can help the reader to gain insight into the worldview being presented and help the writer to better understand the totality of the communication he is making.

As we have suggested earlier, the artifacts of both elite culture and popular culture are equally accessible to rhetorical analysis and seem very little different from one another in terms of their rhetorical content. In fact, whenever elite culture becomes popular or popular culture becomes elite, the difficulty of drawing boundaries seems clear, particularly when we are dealing with writing that is generally described only as "fiction"—one novel resembles another, and the ways of defining elite and popular examples seem vague. However, when we move into the areas of genre, the distinctions are more obvious.

An author may write a novel for any number of reasons, and a useful method of interpretation is that outlined in Booth's *Rhetoric of Fiction*. But generic books are another matter: by being mysteries or romances or fantasies or westerns, they are easily identifiable as popular culture. Certain restraints are imposed upon their composition and certain conventions are expected of them by their readers. Writing generically establishes certain bonds between author, work, and reader at the outset—externally, as it were—that non-generic works (novels) can only establish individually and internally; the bonds are unique to the specific work rather than to the genre to which the work belongs. Nonetheless they are the same kinds of bonds.

Readers select popular fiction according to taste, occasion, and judgment. There is little point in trying to argue the merit of one genre over another in popular fiction. Tastes in science fiction, mystery, romance, or any other genre are not dependent on standards of quality or informed opinion—they probably derive from habits, experiences, and attitudes which were a long time in forming. Perhaps the mystery fan enjoys the puzzle, the deduction, of the mystery form, while the fantasy fan enjoys the unreality, the suspension of the rules of the physical universe, of the fantasy form.

Occasion influences reading selection by virtue of the fact that people read different kinds of books under different circumstances. For example, someone might read a difficult or complex book related to his profession early in the day, when he needs to concentrate, and then read a light, pleasurable book late at night when he is relaxing and retiring. The occasion is linked to the reader's reason for reading, not the writer's reason for writing—if I want to be informed about current theories of rhetoric or want to do some background reading as preparation for a class lecture, I would select different works and read them in different circumstances than if I wanted to be entertained or to be diverted or to read for relaxation—the books I keep by my bed are generally different from the books I keep in my office.

Judgment, the response we most relate to literary criticism, draws upon certain standards of evaluation derived from the reader's background just as taste is, but judgment is not merely the application of some universal scale. It is a personal reaction as well. My response to Paul Scott's novel about the British in India, *The Jewel in the Crown*, is different from a friend's because I evaluate it on its prose style and narrative technique and she evaluates it on its sociological and anthropological accuracy. Judgment is informed by a whole range of influences, including one's own aesthetic, social, ethical, and political beliefs. It can meet taste halfway by discriminating among works for the pleasure they are expected to provide and the conventions they are likely to follow. In terms of generic fiction the success of individual works is likely to lie in the ways they manipulate conventions. All three aspects of response are, of course, interactive, and all three respond to the rhetorical appeals of the individual work.

While much fiction is not dependent on genre as a shaping influence, modes of popular fiction are. A work like Judith Guest's *Ordinary People* is organized around its own internal logic; it shares certain facets of structure with other popular novels by virtue of its being centered on a family crisis and its being narrative—Guest has not had to invent the novel to tell her story—but beyond such general conventions of storytelling which apply to virtually any narrative work and beyond the consistent realism which binds it to a class of novel without defining it very specifically as a literary work, it is little influenced by constraints imposed by generic conventions.

By contrast, a novel like John Le Carre's *The Little Drummer Girl*, no matter how insightfully it analyzes some aspects of the human condition, still needs to provide certain elements—there must be spies, the threat of acts of sabotage or espionage, an atmosphere of deception and danger; without these elements the novel is not a novel of espionage—it becomes something else and thus alters the writer's intentions and the reader's expectations.

In popular fiction genres, consideration of mode influences the ethos, pathos, and logos of individual works and determines the standards of measurement by which they are evaluated. For example, in the genre of mystery novels certain elements need to be present. There needs to be a mystery, a criminal, and a detective. The ways in which these elements are handled are determined not only by the author's worldview, implicit in every work of literature and also in the attraction of certain genres for individual writers, but also by the subgenre in which the author is operating. Mystery novels fall into several subcategories, such as the police procedural, the puzzle, and the hard-boiled detective novel, and these impose further limitations upon the creation and appreciation of the work.

The subgenre determines the logos of the book—the argument or, in the case of the mystery novel, the detection. In a puzzle mystery the emphasis is on the circumstances of the crime and the ingenuity of the detective. Locked-room mysteries, in which the victim is found murdered in a location from which the murderer could not possibly have committed the crime and then escaped, are a prime example of the puzzle form. The working out of the mystery conventionally demands that all clues have been provided for the reader as well as the detective—in some books, particularly those by Ellery Queen, an opportunity is even provided for the reader to guess the solution before the detective explains it all. Since the emphasis in the

book is on the puzzle, the success of the book's logos is tied to
its possibility and its ingenuity, not its verisimilitude or probability. The mysteries of Agatha Christie, Nicholas Blake, Edmund Crispin, Dorothy Sayers, and others in this subcategory
have to follow this logos.

In a police procedural the emphasis is on the methodology
of the police and the reactions of the policemen to their assignment. Logos here is tied to authenticity and verisimilitude—
while there is still a mystery, its baffling features don't strain
credibility and the solution to the mystery is one which can be
arrived at by careful, methodical investigation, not brilliant
flashes of insight. The reader follows the investigation from the
discovery of the crime through preliminary explanations of the
events to the elimination of suspects and the apprehension of
the culprit. By contrast, the puzzle mystery is more concerned
with distracting the reader from the solution to the last possible
moment—surprise is more important to its logos than to that
of the police procedural; consequently a large part of the puzzle mystery is devoted to producing alternative solutions while
the police procedural may discover the killer's identity very early
on and concentrate on the means of apprehension. Georges
Simenon's books about Inspector Maigret, Maj Sjöwall and Per
Wahlöö's novels about Martin Beck, and Ed McBain's series
about the 87th Precinct are good examples of the police procedural.

As a third example of logos determined by subgenre, we turn
to the hard-boiled detective novel. The emphasis here is less
on the procedures or the puzzle and more on the character of
the private detective. While the mystery may be ingenious, the
working out of the solution very often comes from incident piled
upon incident, particularly those involving threats to the detective. In the hard-boiled school people are generally apt to be
more violent than in the puzzle mystery, and the motives by
which they operate are more mundane, worldly, and less ex-
otic than in the puzzle mystery. The logos centers on the experience of the detective; the works of Dashiell Hammett, Raymond Chandler, and Ross MacDonald are classic examples.

What I've been saying about the logos of mystery subgenres
suggests distinctions in pathos and ethos as well. That is, the

pathetic appeal in a puzzle mystery is to the reader's sense of fun, delight in befuddlement, appreciation of the author's ingenuity. The appeal in a police procedural is to an audience more interested in realism and authenticity. The hard-boiled detective novel appeals to an audience which is more cynical and more romantic than those who prefer the other kinds of mysteries; the private detective, more than the amateur sleuth of the puzzle mystery or the policeman of the police procedural, is heroic, the contemporary equivalent of a crusading knight or roving cowboy. Thus the appeal to the audience grows directly out of the mode and is directly tied to the logos.

The pathetic appeal is tied directly, as well, to the triangle of response. A reader's taste and judgment are linked to mode, but the mode determines the kind of taste and judgment the writer needs to appeal to. While it is possible for subgenres to mix, their appeal to an audience is apt to be limited to one genre or another. For example, in *The Locked Room*, Maj Sjöwall and Per Wahlöö confronted their police detective hero, Martin Beck, with a situation out of a puzzle mystery, a murder in a locked room. Yet the novel remains a police procedural (as well as a wry comment on puzzle mysteries) by making the circumstances and motive of the crime perfectly mundane and the solution to be unexpected but perfectly credible—the mystery is less a product of the killer's fiendish ingenuity than a result of sheer happenstance, and the detective's ability to solve the crime depends less on his own imaginative genius than on his determined investigation of probable cause and effect.

This is not to limit the detectives in subgenres of the mystery novel to specific roles—detectives in puzzle mysteries are often Scotland Yard inspectors, some novels about police detectives are every bit as hard boiled as a private-eye mystery, and some private-eye mysteries attempt to be as methodical and authentic as a police procedural or as arch and ingenious as a puzzle mystery. The role of the detective is not the determinant of the subgenre—a puzzle mystery set in a police station and lacking the procedural element is a puzzle mystery, not a police procedural. It is the subgenre that determines the role of the detective, and the appeal to the audience changes with the subgenre, not the detective's role.

Obviously all these elements are tightly bound together. The ethos created in a mystery novel is determined by its subgenre, but the logos it establishes, by the kind of pathos it generates. The ethos of a mystery novel involves both the character of the detective and, perhaps more importantly, the atmosphere of the novel. These are tightly bound together. In the case of the traditional first-person narrative of some forms of the detective novel—Dr. Watson's recounting the adventures of Sherlock Holmes, Archie Goodwin detailing the cases of Nero Wolfe, Philip Marlowe, or the Continental Op or Lew Archer narrating their own adventures—the ethos of the book is established by the simultaneous creation of character and atmosphere.

Ethos is created in a novel from the very first word. The personality not simply of the major character but of the work itself is establshed in the opening paragraphs. We can see the difference in ethos in two different works by comparing their opening passages. The first is from *Frequent Hearses* by Edmund Crispin:

Taking Piccadilly Circus as your centre, draw a circle of radius eighteen miles, and you will find the major film studios—Denham, Elstree, and the rest—dotted about its circumference. Long Fulton lies to the north-west. Should you wish to travel to Long Fulton from Oxford, your best plan is to entrain for London, and on arrival there set out afresh from Marylebone. The cross-country journey is prolonged and tedious, involving four changes—at stations of progressively diminishing size and increasing antiquity, so that the effect is of witnessing a dramatised History of the Railways in reverse—and, in the upshot, a ruinous, draughty single-decker motor-bus. It is advisable, as a general rule, not to attempt this. That Gervase Fen persisted in doing so may be attributed first to his innate perversity and secondly to the fact that the spring season commonly made him torpid, so that to meander through the burgeoning March countryside at twenty miles an hour was an occupation which consorted well with his mood. By getting up at six he could be at Long Fulton comfortably by ten, the time at which script conferences were usually advertised to begin. And since in actual fact (the making of films being what it is) they never began until ten-thirty or eleven, there was ample opportunity for him to drink coffee in the canteen or to rove through the congeries of decrepit-looking structures in which the brain-children of the Leiper Combine were nursed from undisciplined infancy up to the final cutting, dubbing, and reduplication which preceded their *debut* on this or that West End screen. The amusement which this afforded Fen was never more than tenuous. He was unable to regard British films as in any way indispensable to the Good Life, and his own temporary responsibility at the studios—which was to provide expert information about the life and works of Alexander Pope—weighed lightly on him in consequence.[3]

We can note several points about the passage above. It is a very long paragraph, over a page in length, and contains some very long sentences and a number of polysyllabic words. The pace is languid, the language arch, suggesting amused disdain and aloofness. The detective, Gervase Fen, is introduced as detached, critical, and above the milieu in which he finds himself—the mystery will involve murder among the cast and crew of the film—and the reader is invited to adopt his attitude, which is also the attitude of the author. There is a spirit of play and satire here which permeates not only the individual novel but the series as a whole.

The Crispin example makes a striking contrast to the opening passage of *Hail to the Chief* by Ed McBain:

They found the bodies in an open ditch on the northernmost extreme of the 87th Precinct. The telephone company had torn up the street early the morning before, to get at the underground cables. The repairmen finished the job by nightfall, when the temperature dropped below freezing. They had covered the ditch with temporary wooden planking, and had erected blinking barriers around the excavation, to keep the motorists away from the long, narrow, covered trench in the earth. Someone had ripped up the planking and dropped the six bodies into the ditch. Two radio-car cops, on routine patrol near the boat basin, spotted the ripped-up sections of planking and flashed their torches into the excavation. The date was January the sixth. The time was three in the morning. By three-ten, Detectives Steve Carella and Bertram Kling were on the scene.[4]

The passage by Crispin has 327 words in ten sentences, an average of thirty-three words a sentence; the McBain passage has nine sentences but only 142 words, an average of 16 words per sentence, half the length of the Crispin passage. Moreover, the

McBain passage is considerably more matter-of-fact, more declarative, more pointed than the Crispin passage, which is more descriptive, more leisurely, more circular. The McBain passage, by its terseness and its common vocabulary is more appropriate to the police procedural form, to which the 87th Precinct mystery series conforms. The Crispin passage, by its archness and its stuffiness, is more appropriate to the puzzle mystery form, to which the Gervase Fen series conforms. Style, in these two passages, is linked both to mode and to ethos, conforming to the first and creating the second.

I don't mean to suggest by this comparison that each mode has one set ethos to which all artifacts in the mode conform. The ethos of each individual book is unique; in a mystery series, while an author may be hoping to reach a particular audience by imitating certain features of an established, successful writer, each author and each series creates its own ethos, sometimes in spite of itself. The 87th Precinct novels by Ed McBain, the Martin Beck novels by Maj Sjöwall and Per Wahlöö, the Van Der Valk novels by Nicholas Freling, the Maigret novels by Georges Simenon all establish a different ethos—partly through distinctive characterization, partly through distinctive atmosphere. One series may emphasize action, another politics, another psychology, another methodology, each while working within the mode of the police procedural.

To demonstrate the ways in which authors working within the same subgenre create unique ethos—and subsequently appeal to different audiences—I want to turn to some examples of the hard-boiled school. *The Big Sleep*, Raymond Chandler's first Philip Marlowe novel, opens with this passage:

It was about eleven o'clock in the morning, mid-October, with the sun not shining and a look of hard wet rain in the clearness of the foothills. I was wearing my powderblue suit, with dark blue shirt, tie, and display handkerchief, black brogues, black wool socks with dark blue clocks on them. I was neat, clean, shaved, and sober, and I didn't care who knew it. I was everything the well-dressed private detective ought to be. I was calling on four million dollars.

The main hallway of the Sternwood Place was two stories high. Over the entrance doors, which would have let in a troop of Indian elephants, there was a broad stained-glass panel showing a knight in dark armor rescuing a lady who was tied to a tree and didn't have any clothes on but some very long and convenient hair. The knight had pushed the vizor of his helmet back to be sociable, and he was fiddling with the knots on the ropes that tied the lady to the tree and not getting anywhere. I stood there and thought that if I lived in the house, I would sooner or later have to climb up there and help him. He didn't seem to be really trying.[5]

In his book on prose style, *Tough, Sweet, and Stuffy,* Walker Gibson characterizes this style as "tough" because of its first-person narration, its use of common vocabulary, its short simple sentences.[6] Notice that the first paragraph has five sentences, averaging sixteen words a sentence, four of which begin with "I was." Notice also the facetiousness of the narrator, laughing at himself for dressing up for the interview, informing us by his attitude not only toward himself but toward the picture in the hallway of the gulf between his surroundings and himself. The passage implies a comparison between the detective and the knight in the window, suggesting that the detective is considerably less chivalrous and more direct than the knight, although by the end of the book he does perform an act equivalent to the knight's.

Chandler creates the ethos of both Philip Marlowe and the novel in general in this opening passage and follows through consistently in the remainder of the book. By and large the series, which consists of seven novels and a handful of short stories, maintains a consistent ethos throughout, although a later novel, *The Long Good-Bye*, is far more sober and less flip, and the final novel, *Playback*, is arguably not a Marlowe novel at all, because the ethos is so different from the earlier novels.

To demonstrate how the ethos an author creates can change from book to book, compare the passage from *The Big Sleep*, where the first person narrator is Philip Marlowe, with the following passage from a Chandler short story, "Pearls Are a Nuisance," where the first person narrator is a detective named Walter Gage:

The address proved to be a seedy hotel, conveniently close to the interurban car tracks and having its entrance adjoining a Chinese laundry. The hotel was upstairs, the steps being covered—in places—

with strips of decayed rubber matting to which were screwed irregular fragments of unpolished brass. The smell of the Chinese laundry ceased about halfway up the stairs and was replaced by a smell of kerosene, cigar butts, slept-in air and greasy paper bags. There was a register at the head of the stairs on a wooden shelf. The last entry was in pencil, three weeks previous as to date, and had been written by someone with a very unsteady hand. I deduced from this that the management was not over-particular.

There was a bell beside the book and a sign reading: MANAGER. I rang the bell and waited. Presently a door opened down the hall and feet shuffled towards me without haste. A man appeared wearing frayed leather slippers and trousers of a nameless color, which had the two top buttons unlatched to permit more freedom to the suburbs of his extensive stomach. He also wore red suspenders, his shirt was darkened under the arms, and elsewhere, and his face badly needed a thorough laundering and trimming.[7]

Here Chandler reverses the voice of *The Big Sleep* example: Walter Gage is a somewhat effete, facetious, and discriminating detective, finding himself in surroundings too crass and crude for his taste. Philip Marlowe would never take so long to describe a scene or speak in so circuitous a fashion.

Chandler himself made a very specific description of the kind of ethos he wanted to create for his detective-hero. In "The Simple Art of Murder," his review of the art of the detective story, he talks about the cruelty and violence of murder that a realist must face, and writes:

Down these mean streets a man must go who is not himself mean, who is neither tarnished nor afraid. The detective in this kind of story must be such a man. He is the hero; he is everything. He must be a complete man and a common man and yet an unusual man. He must be, to use a rather weathered phrase, a man of honor. . . . [8]

In this famous passage Chandler spells out the particular nature of his hero, and the subsequent writers who have sought to capture the essential qualities of Chandler's work have had to deal with their own concept of the private detective as a tough guy with a code of honor.

Chandler's novels about Philip Marlowe are tales of a man doggedly pursuing the truth, a man occasionally flip, occasionally violent, but never callous, never cruel. There is something of the quality of a questing knight in the character of Marlowe and the comparison at the opening of *The Big Sleep* is apt: whatever their differences, Marlowe too is a hero struggling with conflicting impulses, but always coming out on the side of honor. This sense of ethos is vital to the series—it is not merely the schtick by which the character is identified but the essense of the character, and to some degree Chandler's appeal to readers is founded not only on his famous prose style but also on his readers' sympathy with a man of honor struggling to make sense of a world essentially lacking in it.

The importance of ethos is clear in comparing Chandler's longest, most complex book, *The Long Good-Bye*, with Robert Altman's film adaptation. The novel ends with a final confrontation between Marlowe and the friend who has betrayed him in which they exchange words and Marlowe, having refused a reconciliation, watches the man depart and then informs the police of his whereabouts. The film ends with Marlowe, sardonically played by Elliott Gould, coldly murdering his former friend, executing him, as it were, for crimes he has gotten away with. Critics are divided about the film, but those who like it best like it because it is true to Robert Altman's vision of the world. It is, however, a betrayal of Chandler's vision; Philip Marlowe would never execute a man—that is not his ethos. Consequently, however satisfying the film is for Altman fans, it is not very satisfying for Chandler fans, at least in so far as it functions as a visual representation of Chandler's worldview.

The ending of Altman's *The Long Good-Bye* resembles the endings of a number of novels by Mickey Spillane, particularly *I, The Jury*, where the detective, Mike Hammer, executes a woman whom he has loved and whom he has found guilty of the murder of one of his friends. The difference in ethos in the two series is instructive. Even the titles reveal the difference. Chandler's titles—*The Big Sleep, Farewell, My Lovely, The Long Good-Bye*—are moody, elegaic, romantic; Spillane's—*I, The Jury, The Big Kill, Vengeance Is Mine, Kiss Me, Deadly, My Gun Is Quick*—are vengeful, violent, cynical, and, since three of the five listed are presumably expressions of the hero-narrator's ethic

and a fourth is spoken to the hero by the woman he incinerates
at the end of the book, self-defining.

The ethos of a Mike Hammer novel is fairly clearly established in the opening passage of *Kiss Me, Deadly*:

All I saw was the dame standing there in the glare of the headlights
waving her arms like a huge puppet and the curse I spit out filled the
car and my own ears. I wrenched the wheel over, felt the rear end
start to slide, brought it out with a splash of power and almost ran up
the side of the cliff as the car fishtailed. The brakes bit in, gouging a
furrow in the shoulder, then jumped to the pavement and held.

Somehow I had managed a sweeping curve around the babe. For a
few seconds she had been living on stolen time because instead of
getting out of the way she had tried to stay in the beam of the headlights. I sat there and let myself shake. The butt that had fallen out of
my mouth had burned a hole in the leg of my pants and I flipped it
out the window. The stink of burned rubber and brake lining hung in
the air like smoke and I was thinking of every damn thing I ever
wanted to say to a harebrained woman so I could have it ready when
I got my hands on her.[9]

The short, harsh words that dominate this passage—glare, curse,
spit, wrenched, splash, bit, gouging, jumped—give a sense of
action and violence to the prose; the words for the woman—
dame, babe, harebrained—and the narrator's feelings—"curse
I spit out," "every damn thing I ever wanted to say," "got my
hands on her"—convey a sense of violence toward women in
keeping with the final images of the book and, in fact, with the
series as a whole, since women are often murdered in the books
or killed by Hammer in the final chapters.

The Mike Hammer books are chiefly about an angry man,
usually made angry by the murder of a friend, who sets out to
avenge murder and to punish wrong-doers; he continually sets
himself above the law. In the conclusion of *I, The Jury* he tells
the murderess: "I'm the jury now, and the judge, and I have a
promise to keep. Beautiful as you are, as much as I almost loved
you, I sentence you to death."[10] That attitude is one that Philip
Marlowe would never hold. In *The Big Sleep* he is an accessory
to murder—he discovers a murder and allows the family of the

murderess to institutionalize her for insanity rather than bring the discovery of the body and the identity of the murderess to the attention of the law. There is retribution in the fate of the murderess, but there is also human sympathy, and the compassion of the detective is a hallmark of his character.

In a sense the ethos of an individual mystery novel or of a series helps define its purpose, the fifth element of rhetoric. That is, it may be the author's purpose in writing a mystery to simply entertain an audience through concocting a puzzle, creating colorful and interesting characters, generating a sense of excitement and confusion, or, more complexly, it may be the author's purpose to demonstrate the ways in which order is restored to a disordered world or sense is made of a bewildering world. Yet, reading various writers within a genre or subgenre one gets a sense that their purposes in writing those similar kinds of stories are quite different—that they also have individual purposes related to their view of the society in which they live or the attitudes they hold about human interaction. Chandler's mysteries express a sorrow about human fraility and corruption, Spillane's express an anger and a desire to strike out. All express some desire to set things right somehow.

As always, ethos, pathos, logos, purpose, and mode are inextricably bound together, each influencing and being influenced by the others. The work that emerges is generated by the interaction of these elements. A rhetorical analysis provides a means for distinguishing among popular genres, differentiating among subgenres, and identifying the specific rhetoric of individual authors or particular works. It helps explain what links one work to another and it helps identify the unique characteristics of individual works. Wayne Booth has used rhetorical analysis to great effect on the works of Fielding, Dickens, Flaubert, and James; and Edward Corbett has collected a variety of essays analyzing a range of authors and works; but, as I hope this chapter has made clear, rhetorical analysis is equally valid when applied to the works of popular fiction. What is true of the mystery, of the works of Chandler, Spillane, McBain, and Crispin, is also true of the romance, of the works of Cartland, Dailey, and Rogers, and of the western, of the works of L'Amour, Grey, Short, and Brand.

Rhetorical analysis also helps to clarify the appeal to readers and the distinctions one ought to be able to make among readers. The appeals to audience that Dickens and George Eliot make are different from the appeals made by James Joyce and Thomas Pynchon—the reader's role is not to judge the literary quality of their works (whatever that means and however that may be done) but to respond to them according to their own taste and judgment. Understanding what that taste and judgment are and what in the work makes those appeals can be obtained through rhetorical analysis. The same may be said for works of popular fiction, which in their rhetorical elements and the dynamics of their relationships with their readers are no different from the artifacts of elite culture. In fact, it would no doubt be instructive to turn the attention of rhetorical analysis to works essentially in the same mode but with separate critical standing to produce a valuable description of what makes them different. Essentially George Orwell has pointed the way in his comparison of Hornung's *The Amateur Cracksman* and Chase's *No Orchids for Miss Blandish* and his reference to the similarity of Chase's book to Faulkner's *Sanctuary*.[11] Rhetorical analyses of books on a continuum of literary stature—Jane Austen, Rosemary Rogers, Barbara Cartland; William Faulkner, Horace McCoy, James Hadley Chase; *Moby Dick*, *The Old Man and the Sea*, *Jaws*—might go a long way toward defining the actual gap between elite and popular literature and make us more appreciative of the rhetorics of popular culture.

# Notes

## CHAPTER 1

1. Dwight Macdonald, "Masscult & Midcult," *Against the American Grain* (New York: Random House, 1962), p. 3.
2. Macdonald, p. 14.
3. Bernard Rosenberg, "Mass Culture in America," *Mass Culture: The Popular Arts in America*, ed. Bernard Rosenberg and David Manning White (New York: Free Press, 1962), pp. 3–4.
4. Russel B. Nye, *The Unembarrassed Muse: The Popular Arts in America* (New York: The Dial Press, 1970), p. v.
5. Macdonald, p. 18.

## CHAPTER 2

1. Edward P. J. Corbett, *Classical Rhetoric for the Modern Student*. 2nd ed. (New York: Oxford University Press, 1971), p. 3.
2. Lane Cooper, ed., *The Rhetoric of Aristotle* (Englewood Cliffs, NJ: Prentice-Hall, 1932), p. 7.
3. Corbett, pp. 3–4.
4. Cooper, p. 1.
5. Ibid., p. 17.
6. James L. Kinneavy, *A Theory of Discourse* (Englewood Cliffs, NJ: Prentice-Hall, 1971), p. 19.
7. Cooper, p. 16.
8. Kinneavy, p. 182.
9. Cooper, p. 8.
10. Ibid., pp. 8–9.

11. Ibid., p. 9.

12. Kinneavy, pp. 48–68.

13. See also James Britton, *et al.*, *The Development of Writing Abilities, 11–18* (London: Macmillan Education, 1975), pp. 74–86.

14. See also Richard Lloyd-Jones, "Primary Trait Scoring," *Evaluating Writing: Describing, Measuring, Judging*, ed. Charles R. Cooper and Lee Odell (Urbana, IL: National Council of Teachers of English, 1977), pp. 33–66.

15. O. B. Hardison, "The Rhetoric of Hitchcock's Thrillers," *Man and the Movies*, ed. W. R. Robinson (Baton Rouge: Louisiana State University Press, 1967), pp. 137–138.

16. Aristotle, *The Rhetorics and Poetics of Aristotle*, introd. Edward P. J. Corbett, tr. W. Rhys Roberts and Ingram Bywater (New York: Modern Library, 1984), p. 248.

17. Hoyt H. Hudson, "Rhetoric and Poetry," *Quarterly Journal of Speech* 10 (April 1924): 154.

18. Marie Hochmuth Nichols, *Rhetoric and Criticism* (Baton Rouge: Louisiana State University Press, 1963), pp. 84–85.

19. Kenneth Burke, *A Rhetoric of Motives* (Englewood Cliffs, NJ: Prentice-Hall, 1950), pp. 43–44.

20. James L. Kinneavy, "Contemporary Rhetoric," *The Present State of Scholarship in Historical and Contemporary Rhetoric*, ed. Winifred Bryant Horner (Columbia: University of Missouri Press, 1983), pp. 170–171.

### CHAPTER 4

1. Walker Gibson, *Tough, Sweet, and Stuffy: An Essay on Modern American Prose Styles* (Bloomington: Indiana University Press, 1966), p. 82.

2. Ibid., pp. 84–85.

### CHAPTER 5

1. Edward P. J. Corbett, *Classical Rhetoric of the Modern Student*, 2nd ed. (New York: Oxford University Press, 1971), p. 65.

2. Michael Arlen, *Thirty Seconds* (Baltimore: Penguin Books, 1981), pp. 181–182.

3. Ibid., pp. 69–70.

4. See Wayne C. Booth, "The Company We Keep: Self-Making in Imaginative Art, Old and New," *Daedalus* 111:4 (Fall 1982): 53–56.

5. Arlen, p. 126.

## CHAPTER 6

1. Neal Gabler, "Different Criticism on TV," *Variety* (December 8, 1982): 75.

2. Neal Gabler, Interview with the author, 23 December 1982.

3. David Denby, Interview with the author, 14 October 1982.

4. "Album Notes," *Guitar Player* 14:3 (March 1980): 126.

5. "Album Picks," *Billboard* (December 15, 1979): 68.

6. Joe Fernbacher, "Up Against the Ozone, Matilda Mother," *Creem* 11:10 (March 1980): 53.

7. *Rolling Stone* 310 (February 7, 1980): 75.

8. Denby, Interview.

9. Arthur Schlesinger, Jr., "Movies: Villainy Among the Proletariat," *Saturday Review* (April 15, 1978): 65.

10. Richard Schickel, "Union Dues," *Time* 111:7 (February 13, 1978): 66.

## CHAPTER 7

1. James L. Kinneavy, *A Theory of Discourse* (Englewood Cliffs, NJ: Prentice-Hall, 1971), pp. 38–39, 60–62.

2. Ibid., p. 61.

3. Ibid., p. 61. But see also the whole of Chapter Three, pp. 73–193.

4. Kinneavy, p. 78.

5. Carl Sagan and E. E. Salpeter, "Particles, Environments, and Possible Ecologies in the Jovian Atmosphere," *Astrophysical Journal Supplement* 32 (December 1976): 737.

6. Carl Sagan, *The Cosmic Connection: An Extraterrestrial Perspective* (1973; reprinted New York: Dell, 1976), p. 87.

7. James S. Trefil, "A Consumer's Guide to Pseudoscience," *Saturday Review* (April 29, 1978): 16.

8. Titles by Erich von Däniken include *Chariots of the Gods?* (1967), *Gods from Outer Space* (1970), *Gold of the Gods* (1973), *Miracles of the Gods* (1975), *Signs of the Gods* (1981), and *Pathways to the Gods* (1982). One of his more successful imitators is W. Raymond Drake, author of *Gods and Spacemen in the Ancient East*, *Gods and Spacemen in the Ancient West*, *Gods and Spacemen in Ancient Israel*, and *Gods and Spacemen Throughout History*. Similar titles include *God Drives a Flying Saucer*, *Jesus—Heir of the Ancient Astronauts*, *The Spaceships of Ezekiel*, and *The Outer Space Connection*. Television specials and series and motion picture versions abound.

9. Chief among these are two books by Ronald Story, *The Space-*

*Gods Revealed* (1976) and *The Guardians of the Universe?* (1980); and chapters in *The Search for Life in the Universe* (1980) by Donald Goldsmith and Tobias Owen, *The Galactic Club: Intelligent Life in Outer Space* (1974) by Ronald N. Bracewell, *Broca's Brain: Reflections on the Romance of Science* (1980) by Carl Sagan, and *Can You Speak Venusian?* (1976) by Patrick Moore.

10. Erich von Däniken, *Chariots of the Gods?: Unsolved Mysteries of the Past* (1968; reprinted New York: Bantam, 1970), p. vii.

11. Ibid., p. 22.

12. Ibid., p. 31.

13. Ibid., p. 17.

14. Ibid., p. 100.

15. Ronald Story, *The Space-Gods Revealed: A Close Look at the Theories of Erich von Däniken* (New York: Harper & Row, 1976), pp. xv-xvi.

16. Sagan, *Connection*, p. ix.

17. Von Däniken, p. 6.

18. Sagan, *Connection*, pp. viii–ix.

19. Von Däniken, pp. 7–12; Carl Sagan, *Cosmos* (New York: Random House, 1980), pp. 5–12.

20. Sagan, *Connection*, p. 9.

21. Von Däniken, pp. 40–41.

22. *The New English Bible with the Apocrypha* (New York: Oxford University Press, 1971).

23. Von Däniken, p. 128.

24. I. S. Shklovskii and Carl Sagan, *Intelligent Life in the Universe* (San Francisco: Holden-Day, 1966), p. 363. On p. 364 Shklovskii and Sagan write: "Phobos is the only known moon in the solar system with a period of revolution about its planet which is less than the period of rotation of the planet itself." Von Däniken writes: "They are the only known moons in our solar system that move around their mother planet faster than she herself rotates" (p. 128).

25. Shklovskii and Sagan, p. 376. Von Däniken is wrong to attribute the theory to Sagan; it is clear in their book that Shklovskii developed it and that Sagan doubts it.

26. Von Däniken, p. 129.

27. Sagan, *Connection*, p. 110.

28. Ibid., p. 111.

29. Ibid., p. 112.

30. Ibid., pp. 112–113.

## CHAPTER 8

1. Aristotle, *The Rhetoric and Poetics of Aristotle*, intro. Edward P. J. Corbett, tr. W. Rhys Roberts and Ingram Bywater (New York: Modern Library, 1984), pp. 31–32.

2. Lane Cooper, ed., *The Rhetoric of Aristotle* (Englewood Cliffs, NJ: Prentice-Hall, 1932), pp. xxxvii, 16–17.

3. Aristotle, pp. 32–33.

4. Richard Reeves, *Jet Lag: The Running Commentary of a Bicoastal Reporter* (Kansas City: Andrews and McMeel, 1981), p. 123.

5. Tom Wicker, *On Press* (New York: Viking, 1978), p. 150.

6. Ibid., p. 155.

7. Richard Reeves, Interview with the author, 8 November 1984.

8. Tom Wicker, Interview with the author, 8 October 1982.

9. Wicker, *Press*, p. 49.

10. Lars-Erik Nelson, "The President Takes Us into the Twilight Zone," *Detroit Free Press* (November 8, 1984): 11A.

11. Anthony Lewis, "You Ain't Seen Nothing Yet," *New York Times* (November 8, 1984): A31.

12. James J. Kilpatrick, "Encore! Reagan's Personal Triumph," *Detroit Free Press* (November 8, 1984): 11A.

13. Lewis, p. A31.

14. Kilpatrick, p. 11A.

15. Nelson, p. 11A.

16. Tom Wicker, "The New Reality," *New York Times* (November 9, 1984): A31.

17. William Safire, "The Prairie Fire," *New York Times* (November 8, 1984): A31.

18. Ibid., p. A31.

## CHAPTER 9

1. David Reisman, "Listening to Popular Music," *Mass Culture: The Popular Arts in America*, ed. Bernard Rosenberg and David Manning White (New York: The Free Press, 1957), pp. 393–403.

2. Particularly James T. Carey, "Changing Courtship Patterns in the Popular Song," *American Journal of Sociology* 74 (May 1969): 720–731; Richard R. Cole, "Top Songs in the Sixties: A Content Analysis of Popular Lyrics," *Mass Communication and Youth: Some Current Perspectives*, ed. F. Gerald Kline and Peter Clarke (Beverly Hills: Sage Publications, 1971), pp. 87–98; Joseph R. Dominick, "The Portable Friend: Peer Group Membership and Radio Usage," *Journal of Broadcasting* 18:2 (Spring 1974): 161–170; Herbert Goldberg, "Contemporary Popular Music," *Journal of Popular Culture* 4:3 (Winter 1971): 579–589; S. I. Hayakawa, "Popular Song vs. The Facts of Life," *Mass Culture: The Popular Arts in America*, pp. 393–403; Donald Horton, "The Dialogue of Courtship in Popular Songs," *American Journal of Sociology* 62:6 (May 1957): 569–578; John Wanzenried and Vincent di Salvo, "Intensional and Extensional Orientations on Rock and Roll Music," *ETC:*

*A Review of General Semantics* 32:1 (March 1975): 31–43; John Wanzen-ried and Robert Henley Woody, "Country and Western Song Lyrics: Intensional and Extensional Orientations," *Popular Music in Society* 5:5 (1977): 89–92.

3. R. Serge Denisoff and Mark H. Levine, "The Popular Protest Songs: The Case of 'Eve of Destruction,'" *Public Opinion Quarterly* (Spring 1971): 11–122.

4. Paul M. Hirsch, "Sociological Approaches to the Pop Music Phenomenon," *Mass Communications and Youth: Some Current Perspectives,* ed. F. Gerald Kline and Peter Clarke (Beverly Hills: Sage Publications, 1971), pp. 69–86.

5. John Lahr, "On-Stage," *Village Voice* 17:8 (February 24, 1972): 56.

6. Walter Gantz, Howard M. Gartenberg, Martin L. Pearson, Seth O. Schiller, "Gratifications and Expectations Associated with Pop Music among Adolescents," *Popular Music in Society* 6:1 (1978): 84.

7. Lahr, p. 56.

8. Bob Reiss, "Linda Ronstadt: When Will I Be Loved?", *The Best of the Post* (New York: Popular Library, 1979), p. 86.

9. "Tonight's the Night" by Rod Stewart. Copyright 1976.

10. "We've Got Tonite" by Bob Seger. Copyright 1976 by Gear Publishing Co.

11. "Desiree" by Neil Diamond. Copyright 1977.

12. "Night Moves" by Bob Seger. Copyright 1976 by Gear Publishing Co.

13. Hirsch, p. 77.

14. "Stayin' Alive" by Barry, Robin, and Maurice Gibb. Copyright 1977 by RSO Records, Inc.

15. "How Deep Is Your Love?" By Barry, Robin, and Maurice Gibb. Copyright 1977 by RSO Records, Inc.

16. "Rhumba Girl (Rhumba Man)" by Jesse Winchester. Copyright 1977 by fourth Floor Music, Inc.; "Angels Rejoiced" by Ira and Charlie Louvin. Copyright 1957 by Central Songs.

**CHAPTER 10**

1. Joel Nydahl, "Thinking and Writing about Television: The Rhetoric of News in the Composition Class," paper presented to the Michigan College English Association, October 26, 1984, pp. 5–6.

2. Ronald Primeau, *The Rhetoric of Television* (New York: Longman, 1979), p. ix.

3. George Orwell, "Charles Dickens," *A Collection of Essays* (New York: Harcourt Brace Jovanovich, 1953), p. 90.

4. Horace Newcomb, "Toward a Television Aesthetic," *Television: The Critical View*, ed. Horace Newcomb (New York: Oxford University Press, 1979), p. 421.

## CHAPTER 11

1. Wayne C. Booth, *The Rhetoric of Fiction* (Chicago: University of Chicago Press, 1961), p. i.

2. George Orwell, "The Proletarian Writer," *The Collected Essays, Journalism and Letters of George Orwell*, volume 2: *My Country Right or Left*, ed. Sonia Orwell and Ian Angus (New York: Harcourt Brace Jovanovich, 1968), p. 41.

3. Edmund Crispin, *Frequent Hearses* (1950; reprinted, Baltimore: Penguin, 1982), pp. 5–6.

4. Ed McBain, *Hail to the Chief* (New York: Random House, 1973), pp. 3–4.

5. Raymond Chandler, *The Big Sleep* (1930; reprinted, Pocket Books, 1950), p. 1.

6. Walker Gibson, *Tough, Sweet and Stuffy: An Essay on Modern American Prose Styles* (Bloomington: Indiana University Press, 1966), pp. 28–42.

7. Raymond Chandler, *The Simple Art of Murder* (1950; reprinted, New York: Ballantine, 1972), p. 169.

8. Chandler, *Simple Art*, p. 20.

9. Mickey Spillane, *Kiss Me, Deadly* (1952; reprinted, New York: New American Library, 1953), p. 7.

10. Mickey Spillane, *I, The Jury* (1947; reprinted, New York: New American Library, 1948), p. 144.

11. George Orwell, "Raffles and Miss Blandish," *The Collected Essays, Journalism, and Letters*, volume 3: *As I Please*, pp. 212–224.

# APPENDIX

# Suggestions for Study

It has been my intention in this book not only to explain the rhetorics of popular culture but also to suggest how rhetorical analysis might profitably be applied to better understand both the ways popular culture communicates and the ways rhetoric functions in the contemporary world. I have attempted, after all, to write a book which is in equal measure a book about rhetoric and a book about popular culture. Consequently, my suggestions for classroom (and to some degree, independent) application all involve extensions of the analyses modeled in individual chapters, either through further rhetorical analysis of various forms of popular culture or through imitation of their rhetorical method. The possibilities are limited only by the imagination of the individual classroom teacher, and, since this book has not attempted to be comprehensive, there are still further areas of advertising, advocacy, and entertainment to which rhetorical analysis might profitably be applied.

## THE RHETORICS OF ADVERTISING

### The Rhetoric of Direct Mail

*Materials*: Subscription letters; assorted magazines.

*Applications*: The unit could be part of larger units analyzing periodicals, examining methods of persuasion, or demonstrating rhetorical elements.

*Steps in the Activity*: Steps 3, 4, 5 can be used as alternatives for one another or in combination to extend the sequence.

1. Introduction: Discuss with students the magazines they have in their homes or have read elsewhere. Which magazines made an impression? Who do they think reads them? What are they like? What elements or features do they have? What kind of person publishes the magazine? How do you know? Suggest that you can tell a lot about a magazine by its letters soliciting subscription.

Provide students with sample subscription letters, preferably those providing clear contrasts: *The Wall Street Journal* and *Mother Jones*, *The Atlantic* and *Esquire*. Discuss the kind of person the author represents himself to be, the kind of magazine he claims to edit or publish, the kind of person the letter suggests the reader is.

2. Group Analysis: Provide the class with three or four more examples and ask them to make some distinctions among them, in writing. Specifically, have them look at the author's persona, the representation of the magazine, and the representation of the reader. Discuss the results of these writings or journal entries and invite students to be specific about the reasons for their choices. You might even ask them to rank the letters from most convincing to least convincing. At this point it would be helpful to make them appreciate the way their own tastes and biases make them more or less receptive to persuasion.

3. Independent Analysis: Give the student the opportunity to compare two more solicitation letters of his or her choice and take it through the composing process. Allow time for prewriting and small group discussion (all students doing similar kinds of magazines in the same group), drafting and revising (preferably in small editing groups), and preparing a final draft. *Variation I*: Have students analyze the letter in a journal entry and compare the letter with an actual copy of the magazine for the formal paper. *Variation II*: Publish the student analyses of the magazine solicitations as a "Class Guide to Current Magazines."

4. Independent Imitation: Give students criteria or ask them to create criteria for analyzing the elements of a magazine, its likely audience, its editorial position. Have them apply the criteria to a magazine of their choice, confirmed by group discussion. Then ask them to write a letter soliciting subscriptions to the magazine. Have them take it through the composing process and possibly publish it. *Variation I*: Have them invent a magazine and write a letter soliciting subscription to it. *Variation II*: Have them write a letter soliciting resubscription or requesting overdue payment. *Variation III*: Have them create an "ideal reader" ad: "What kind of person reads X? Someone who . . . "

5. Personal Application: Have the students each select a magazine they would like to subscribe to and write an essay describing the magazine, its features and perspective, its readership, and explaining why it's a magazine for them as individuals. *Variation*: Have the student select a friend or relative to whom to give a gift subscription and have her justify the appropriateness of the magazine for the person she chooses by the description and explanation paper above.

## The Rhetoric of Print Advertising

*Materials*: Print ads culled from a variety of magazines and newspapers; students may each provide several from home publications for greater variety.

1. Introduction: Discuss the rhetoric of print advertising with the class, emphasizing the rhetorical elements and comparing various examples.

2. Group Analysis: Divide the class into small groups. Give the students time to analyze a cluster of advertisements together and report on their findings. This might take the form of simple in-class discussion with end-of-class reports back to the whole class. (Opaque projector or slide projector presentation of ads under discussion would be useful here.)

3. Independent Analysis: Let students find two or three ads of the same brand or of competing brands of a specific product. Let them write a comparative rhetorical analysis of those ads, emphasizing the differences in the appeals being made. *Variation I*: The independent analysis might well be presented in class as an oral presentation. *Variation II*: The independent analysis might fruitfully be tested first by presentation to the small group members with suggestions for modification and/or addition coming from other students.

4. Independent Imitation: Either provide for students or let students provide for themselves pictures from ads or illustrations to serve as the pictorial content for a print advertisement of the student's own design. Each student is to imagine the product, the physical composition of the ad, and the text to accompany the illustration, and create the print advertisement.

5. Group Imitation: Let the group invent a product, decide on various markets for it, and collectively produce a campaign in which their individual imitations relate to a large overall marketing plan. *Variation I*: Any of the imitations might profitably be a print ad for a product advertised earlier in a direct mail unit.

## The Rhetoric of Television Commercials

*Materials*: If your school has a video cassette recorder you should collect a number of commercials from current programs for class showings. Local television stations might be willing to lend commercials to the school. Each year films are produced collecting the Clio Award winners for best commercials and are available for commercial rental or purchase. (If feasible, a field trip to a local television station to hear programmers discuss commercials, to watch commercials being telecast, and to preview commercials for various time slots would be highly profitable for students.)

1. Introduction: Whether accompanied by an in-class showing or not, provide the student with a scene-by-scene analysis of a particularly well-known commercial, including all its elements—dialogue, cinematography, music, voiceover. Help them to understand the dynamics of the commercial as a rhetorical form.

2. Analysis: Ask individual students to provide similar scene-by-scene descriptions of commercials they are particularly familiar with. Allow them time to discuss their descriptions in small groups and compare their ideas about the rhetorical content of each commercial. Then ask them to write up the description and attach a formal analysis of its rhetorical content. *Variation I*: For schools with VCR equipment, students could tape commercials, show them in class, and present oral reports on their rhetoric. Or—*Variation II*: In a more ambitious project students could tape their oral reports individually and edit them onto tapes of the commercials under discussion for in-class showing, permanent classroom samples, and/or parent-teacher open house displays.

3. Imitation: With transcripts of professional commercials as examples, students can invent their own products or use existing ones and write their own shooting scripts. *Variation I*: Students could work as a group to write and tape their own commercials.

## THE RHETORIC OF ADVOCACY

### The Rhetoric of Reviewing

*A. A Guide to Current Television Series: Review Writing Assignment*

1. Together with the class create a form for reporting on television series. (Possible spaces: Title, Network, Time, and Day, Continuing Actors and Their Roles, Explanations of Relationships between Con-

tinuing Characters, Explanations of Plots of Two Separate Episodes, Positive Elements, Negative Elements, Summary Statement/Reviewer Evaluation.)

2. Make up the forms. Divide the class into small groups according to genre: adventure, mystery, situation comedy, drama/melodrama, etc. Have students name as many series in each category as possible, then let them select one series apiece to review.

3. Allow time for students to have seen two episodes of the series. Reconvene the groups. Have them discuss their conclusions about the series they're reporting on and the reasons for their conclusions.

4. Assign them to write page-and-a-half to two-page double-spaced summaries of their conclusions, including evidence drawn from the report forms about relationships, typical plots, and positive/negative elements.

5. Ask each student to revise the summary and prepare a two-page single-spaced review with factual information about the show (title, network, telecast time, cast) followed by the text of their response summaries.

6. Duplicate, collate, and bind class reviews with a title page and table of contents. Consider school wide distribution. (*Note*: The assignment would be of particular interest in the fall, when new series debut. With a few changes, the assignment would work as well with movies, books, or recordings.)

*B. A Guide to Current Movies: Review Analysis Assignment*

1. Announce the purpose of the assignment: to create an anthology of summaries of critical opinions about current films. Prepare a list of new, recent, and upcoming releases and allow students to select their own choices for study. Be sure films are important enough to have been widely reviewed.

2. Set a limit on the number of screen credits to be recorded and the minimal number of reviews to be read.

3. Provide students with sample reviews for in-class analyses. Ask them to determine what a critic thinks about a film and what evidence the critic offers in support of his or her opinion.

4. Review library and research skills and provide likely sources for reviews.

5. Once students have had time for research, allow time in class for small group discussion of findings, letting class members help with analysis of vague reviews or the synthesis of varying reviews.

6. Ask for a draft synthesizing the reviews the student has read and summarizing the judgment of the critics. Have students discuss revision either in conference with you or in small group revision sessions.

7. Have students prepare a two-page single-spaced final draft including screen credits, a one- or two-word summary of critical response ("See It," "Shun It," "Mixed Reviews") for the upper right-hand corner, and the text of their analytical summary.

8. Reproduce, collate, and distribute the guide as in the other assignment.

## THE RHETORIC OF SPECULATION

*Goal*: An anthology of student writing exploring the validity of evidence in some area of pseudoscience.

1. Selection: Break the class into small groups and let them choose a topic to explore. In a book like *Chariots of the Gods?* each group might approach a single chapter or issue, Group A taking pyramids; Group B, Easter Island; Group C, Nasca lines; Group D, cave drawing; and so on. Or each group might attempt to explore a different pseudoscience topic, ancient astronauts, lost continents, psychic phenomena, supernatural manifestations, etc. In either case the group should further subdivide the topic so that each person has a limited area of inquiry.

2. Prewriting: Class sessions should allow group members to share their findings with one another, explore together their discoveries, examine one another's sources, compare notes and responses to outside material. Together their discussion will allow them time to think through concepts and ideas and begin to brainstorm possible approaches to the paper. A class session should be set aside for students to help each other establish the central ideas and organization of their papers.

3. Writing: Allow a class session for discussion of work in progress, checking through development, organization, unity, clarity, the whole group assisting each of its members to arrive at a clear, solidly supported text.

4. Editing and proofreading: Once the group is satisfied that the papers are logically and stylistically sound, a final reading for editorial purposes can be held, dwelling on mechanics and forms.

5. Extensions: The entire class effort can be duplicated and bound as a publication for the class. The papers can serve as the basis for oral reports on these subjects. The anthology might be sold in the school or community and a different subject might be explored annually for publication.

## THE RHETORIC OF OPINION

Discussion of political columns in the local daily paper can be a stimulating way to keep students in touch with current issues and also reinforce the need for rhetorical analysis. In class discussion of newspaper columns over a period of time, including comparison of columns essentially on the same issues, can sharpen students' perceptions about the rhetoric of opinion. Assignments might ask students to:

1. Analyze two or more columnists dealing with the same issue.
2. Analyze several columns over a period of weeks by the same columnist and produce an overview of the author's work. (This might be done either by assigning columnists to individuals in the class or by letting individuals in a group analyze separate columns by the same writer and then collaborate on an introduction to the analyses or a general overview of the author's work with specific references.)
3. Imitate (ghostwrite a column for) a specific author.
4. Parody political columns.
5. Create a political column of one's own on school, community, and public affairs.

## THE RHETORICS OF ENTERTAINMENT

### The Rhetoric of Popular Music

After being introduced to the rhetoric of popular music with classroom examples, students should be given practice in rhetorical analysis.

1. Group Analysis: Provide students with lyrics and play an album they are reasonably unlikely to have encountered although, preferably, it is a recent release. Ask them individually to analyze the record rhetorically, separating their personal reactions from their analytical reactions. Then ask them to compare notes as a group and collaborate on a brief review of the record. Duplicate the reviews and discuss them comparatively in class.

2. Individual Analysis: Ask students to then apply rhetorical analysis to an album of their own choosing, stressing that any judgments they make must be supported by evidence—specific references to individual songs, words, melodies, arrangements—and that first and foremost their analyses ought to be descriptive of the record's "rhetoric" and the description ought to be well-substantiated. (See also the assignments under "The Rhetoric of Reviewing.")

### THE RHETORIC OF TELEVISION

After being introduced to the rhetoric of television drama with classroom examples, students should be given practice in rhetorical analysis.

1. Group analysis: Either by genre or by individual selection students should take one individual program to analyze, concentrating first on the opening credits and then on the way the individual episode supports or contradicts the credits. After group discussion, students could write up individual analyses, taken through the composing process with the group.

2. Individual analysis: Students could select individual shows to analyze, along the lines discussed in Chapter 10.

3. Creative alternatives: Students could select individual shows to watch without seeing the credits and attempt to generate shooting scripts of the credits of those programs. A follow-up assignment could let them compare their imagined credits with the actual ones used. *Variation I*: Students could script the credits for a series based on their lives or daily in their community or school. *Variation II*: Where equipment is available, students could videotape the credits for their own series. (See also the assignments under "The Rhetoric of Reviewing.")

## THE RHETORIC OF POPULAR FICTION

Introduce the topic of the rhetoric of popular fiction by a close reading of an individual book and/or examination of comparative excerpts, such as those in Chapter 11. You might turn to work you have already covered (*A Tale of Two Cities*) or examples relevant to the course (two first person narratives by Edgar Allan Poe; excerpts from *Walden* and *Life on the Mississippi*) or material of interest to your particular students (the opening sections of *Old Yeller*, *The Yearling*, and *Where the Red Fern Grows*). Give the students the opportunity to practice rhetorical analysis in various assignments as well as in one expressly rhetorical exercise; thinking about fiction in a rhetorical way is a useful critical approach to cultivate.

1. Group Work on the Rhetoric of Genres: Let students select among popular genres (westerns, mysteries, science-fiction, fantasy, Gothic, romance, etc.). Samples can be had cheaply at local used paperback stores. Divide them into groups by genre to read, discuss, and compile rhetorical analyses of their reading. Let them collaborate on an introduction to the genre and individually contribute two or more reviews of individual books. Collect and publish the introductions and reviews as a rhetorical guide to popular fiction.

2. Comparative Rhetorical Analyses: *Compare similar works.* Invite students to write comparative rhetorical analyses of the opening sections of two or more books, preferably traditional as well as contemporary fiction, and perhaps emphasizing first-person narration. Likely comparisons might include *David Copperfield* with *Huckleberry Finn*, *Jane*

*Eyre* with *Pride and Prejudice, Moby Dick* with *The Heart of Darkness, A Clockwork Orange* with *Riddley Walker, Little Women* with *Little House on the Prairie, Anne of Green Gables* with *Rebecca of Sunnybrook Farm, Black Beauty* with *The Black Stallion.*

*Compare the works of a single author.* By comparing the opening passages or selections of several works by the same author, the student could write a paper in which he collates and synthesizes primary research, first by providing analyses of the individual works, second by synthesizing his analyses into a general overview of the author's work. For example, this approach would help reveal the similarities and differences in the works of a single author like Jane Austen, Louisa May Alcott, Mark Twain, and others. Likely comparisons: *Tom Sawyer, Huckleberry Finn, The Prince and the Pauper; Pride and Prejudice, Northanger Abbey, Emma; Oliver Twist, David Copperfield, Great Expectations.*

3. Imitation or Parody of a Generic Work: Assign students to write an imitation or parody of a generic work. (You might compare a passage from Hemingway's *Across the River and Into the Trees* with E. B. White's "Across the Street and Into the Grill" as an illustration of how parody works.) Students might be divided into small discussion/editing groups on the basis of their genre or intentions. A variation might allow imitations, parodies, *or* analyses and collect all three for a class anthology on popular genres. A bulletin board in the school might post photocopies of original passages and student imitations and parodies, an invitation to creativity and further reading. This assignment also lends itself to oral reading activities. You might tie the assignment of imitation or parody to the literature the course focuses on, if any (stories by Poe, Twain, Hawthorne; poetry by Wordsworth, Keats, Shelley, and so on).

4. Instructions in How to Write Generic Fiction: Students might be allowed to write essays giving instructions on how to write a book in a specific genre, focusing on the rhetorical elements. (Have this kind of ethos represented by this kind of persona; this kind of pathos achieved by this kind of scene; this kind of logos accomplished by this kind of plot.) The instructions ought to have examples and illustrations drawn from or modelled on actual books. A series of bulletin boards might post the best how-to essays together with passages and pages from typical works, another entertaining and thought-provoking display. A variation might add the best of these kinds of how-to essays with imitations and parodies from Option 3, all bound in a classroom anthology.

# Select Bibliography on Popular Culture

Arlen, Michael J. *The Living Room War*. New York: Viking, 1969.
———. *Thirty Seconds*. New York: Farrar, Straus & Giroux, 1980.
———. *The View from Highway One: Essays on Television*. New York: Farrar, Straus & Giroux, 1976.
Arnheim, Rudolph. *Film as Art*. Berkeley: University of California Press, 1957.
Aronowitz, Stanley. *False Promises: The Shaping of American Working Class Consciousness*. New York: McGraw-Hill, 1973.
Aronson, James. *The Press and the Cold War*. Indianapolis: Bobbs-Merrill, 1970.
Atwan, Robert, Barry Orton, and William Vesterman, eds. *American Mass Media: Industries and Issues*. New York: Random House, 1978.
Baker, Samm. *The Permissible Lie: The Inside Truth About Advertising*. Boston: Beacon, 1971.
Baker, Stephen. *Visual Persuasion*. New York: McGraw-Hill, 1961.
Barnouw, Erik. *Tube of Plenty: The Evolution of American Television*. New York: Oxford University Press, 1975.
Berger, Arthur Asa. *The Comic-Stripped American*. Baltimore: Penguin Books, 1974.
Boorstein, Daniel. *The Americans: The Democratic Experience*. New York: Random House, 1973.
———. *The Image: A Guide to Pseudo-Events in America*. New York: Atheneum, 1964.
Bosmajian, Haig. *The Language of Oppression*. Washington: Public Affairs Press, 1974.

Buzzi, Giancarlo. *Advertising: Its Cultural and Political Effects*. Minneapolis: University of Minnesota Press, 1967.

Carpenter, Edmund, and Marshall McLuhan, eds. *Explorations in Communication*. Boston: Beacon, 1960.

Casty, Alan, ed. *Mass Media and Mass Man*. New York: Holt, Rinehart, Winston, 1968.

Cater, Douglass, and Richard Adler, eds. *Television as a Cultural Force*. New York: Praeger, 1976.

Cawelti, John. *Adventure, Mystery, and Romance: Formula Stories as Art and Popular Culture*. Chicago: University of Chicago Press, 1976.

————. *The Six-Gun Mystique*. Bowling Green, OH: Bowling Green University Popular Press, 1973.

Crouse, Timothy. *The Boys on the Bus*. New York: Random House, 1973.

Deer, Irving, and Harriet A. Deer. *The Popular Arts: A Critical Reader*. New York: Scribners, 1967.

Denby, David, ed. *Awake in the Dark: An Anthology of American Film Criticism, 1915 to the Present*. New York: Vintage, 1977.

English, John. *Criticizing the Critics* (Humanistic Studies in the Communications Arts). New York: Hastings House, 1979.

Epstein, Edward Jay. *News from Nowhere: Television and the News*. New York: Random House, 1973.

Fishwick, Marshall, and Ray B. Browne, eds. *Icons of Popular Culture*. Bowling Green, OH: Bowling Green University Press, 1970.

Fox, Stephen. *The Mirror Makers: A History of American Advertising and Its Creators*. New York: William Morrow, 1984.

Gans, Herbert. *Popular Culture and High Culture: An Analysis and Evaluation of Taste*. New York: Basic Books, 1974.

Goldstein, Richard. *The Poetry of Rock*. New York: Bantam, 1969.

Gurko, Leo. *Heroes, Highbrows, and the Popular Mind*. Indianapolis: Bobbs-Merrill, 1953.

Hall, James B., and Barry Ulanov, eds. *Modern Culture and the Arts*. New York: McGraw Hill, 1967.

Hammel, William M., ed. *The Popular Arts in America: A Reader*, 2nd ed. New York: Harcourt, Brace, Jovanovich, 1977.

Heilbroner, Robert L. "Advertising as Agitprop: Puncturing the Myths about Hype," *Harper's Magazine* 270 (January 1985): 71–76.

Hoggart, Richard. *The Uses of Literacy: Aspects of Working Class Life with Special Reference to Publications and Entertainment*. New York: Oxford University Press, 1970.

Johnson, Nicholas. *How to Talk Back to Your Television Set*. Boston: Little, Brown, 1970.

Kael, Pauline. *Deeper into Movies*. Boston: Little, Brown, 1973.

————. *I Lost It at the Movies*. New York: Bantam, 1966.

Kahane, Howard. *Logic and Contemporary Rhetoric: The Use of Reason in Everyday Life*. Belmont: Wadsworth, 1976.

Kerr, Walter. *Tragedy and Comedy*. New York: Simon & Schuster, 1967.

Knight, Arthur. *The Liveliest Art: A Panoramic History of the Movies*. New York: Macmillan, 1957.

Krugman, Herbert E. "The Impact of Television Advertising: Learning Without Involvement," *Public Opinion Quarterly* 29 (1965): 349–356.

Landrum, Larry, Pat Browne, and Ray B. Browne, eds. *Dimensions of Detective Fiction*. Bowling Green, OH: Popular Press, 1976.

Lasch, Christopher. *The Culture of Narcissim: American Life in an Age of Diminishing Expectations*. New York: W. W. Norton, 1978.

Lowenthal, Leo. *Literature, Popular Culture and Society*. Palo Alto, CA: Pacific Books, 1968.

Macdonald, Dwight. *Against the American Grain*. New York: Random House, 1962.

Mander, Jerry. *Four Arguments for the Elimination of Television*. New York: William Morrow, 1977.

Marcus, Greil. *Mystery Train: Images of America in Rock 'n' Roll Music*. New York: E. P. Dutton, 1975.

McGinniss, Joe. *The Selling of the President 1968*. New York: Trident, 1969.

McLuhan, Marshall. *The Gutenberg Galaxy: The Making of Typographic Man*. Toronto: University of Toronto, Press, 1962.

————. *Understanding Media: The Extensions of Man*. New York: Mc-Graw-Hill, 1964.

————., and Quentin Fiore. *The Medium Is the Massage*. New York: Bantam, 1967.

McQuade, Donald, and Robert Atwan. *Popular Writing in America: The Interaction of Style and Audience*, 3rd ed. New York: Oxford University Press, 1985.

Metz, Christian. *Language and Cinema*. The Hague: Mouton, 1974.

Newcomb, Horace., ed. *Television: The Critical View*. 2nd ed. New York: Oxford University Press, 1979.

————. *TV: The Most Popular Art*. New York: Anchor, 1974.

Nye, Russel. *The Unembarrassed Muse: The Popular Arts in America*. New York: The Dial Press, 1970.

Ohlgren, Thomas H., and Lynn M. Berk, eds. *The New Languages: A Rhetorical Approach to the Mass Media and Popular Culture*. Englewood Cliffs: Prentice-Hall, 1977.

Palmer, Tony. *All You Need Is Love: The Story of Popular Music*. New York: Grossman, 1976.

Reeves, Richard. *Jet Lag: The Running Commentary of a Bicoastal Reporter*. Kansas City: Andrews & McMeel, 1981.

Rissover, Frederick, and David C. Birch. *Mass Media and the Popular Arts*. New York: McGraw-Hill, 1971.

Rosenberg, Bernard, and David Manning White, eds. *Mass Culture: The Popular Arts in America*. New York: Free Press, 1959.

Schudson, Michael. *Advertising: The Uneasy Persuasion—Its Dubious Impact on American Society*. New York: Basic Books, 1984.

————. *Discovering the News: A Social History of American Newspapers*. New York: Basic Books, 1978.

Seldes, Gilbert. *The Public Arts*. New York: Simon & Schuster, 1956.

Smith, Robert Rutherford. *Beyond the Wasteland: The Criticism of Broadcasting*. Falls Church, VA: Speech Communication Skills, 1976.

Toffler, Alvin. *Future Shock*. New York: Random House, 1970.

Tuchman, Gaye, Arlene Kaplan Daniels, and James Benet. *Hearth and Home: Images of Women in the Mass Media*. New York: Oxford University Press, 1978.

Warshow, Robert. *The Immediate Experience: Movies, Comics, Theatre, & Other Aspects of Popular Culture*. Garden City: Doubleday, 1964.

White, David Manning, and Richard Averson. *The Celluoid Weapon: Social Comment in the American Film*. Boston: Beacon, 1972.

Wicker, Tom. *On Press*. New York: Viking, 1978.

Wills, Gary. *Lead Time: A Journalist's Education*. Garden City: Doubleday, 1983.

Wise, David. *The Politics of Lying: Government Deception, Secrecy, and Power*. New York: Random House, 1973.

# Select Bibliography on Rhetoric

Aristotle. *The Rhetoric of Aristotle*, tr. Lane Cooper. New York: Appleton-Century-Crofts, 1960.

Augustine. *On Christian Doctrine*, tr. D. W. Robertson. Indianapolis: Bobbs-Merrill, 1958.

Bailey, Dudley, ed. *Essays on Rhetoric*. New York: Oxford University Press, 1965.

Baldwin, Charles. *Ancient Rhetoric and Poetic*. New York: Crowell-Collier and Macmillan, 1924.

———. *Medieval Rhetoric and Poetic*. New York: Crowell-Collier and Macmillan, 1928.

Benson, Thomas W., and Michael H. Prosser, eds. *Readings in Classical Rhetoric*. Bloomington, IN: Indiana University Press, 1972.

Bitzer, Lloyd, and Edwin Black, eds. *The Prospect of Rhetoric*. Englewood Cliffs, NJ: Prentice-Hall, 1971.

Booth, Wayne. *Modern Dogma and the Rhetoric of Assent*. Chicago: University of Chicago Press, 1974.

———. *The Rhetoric of Fiction*. Chicago: University of Chicago Press, 1961.

———. "The Rhetorical Stance," *College Composition and Communication* 14 (October 1963): 139–145.

Braddock, Richard, Richard Lloyd-Jones, and Lowell Shorer. *Research in Written Composition*. Urbana, IL: National Council of Teachers of English, 1963.

Bryant, Donald C., ed. *Papers in Rhetoric and Poetic*. Iowa City: University of Iowa Press, 1965.

———. *Rhetorical Dimensions in Criticism*. Baton Rouge: Louisiana State University Press, 1973.

————. *The Rhetorical Idiom: Essays in Rhetoric, Oratory, Language, and Drama*. Ithaca, NY: Cornell University Press, 1958.

Burke, Edmund. *A Philosophical Enquiry into the Origins of Our Ideas of the Sublime and Beautiful*, ed. J. T. Boulton. New York: Columbia University Press, 1958.

Burke, Kenneth. *A Rhetoric of Motives*. Englewood Cliffs, NJ: Prentice-Hall, 1950.

Burks, Don M., ed. *Rhetoric, Philosophy, and Literature: An Exploration*. West Lafayette, IN: Purdue University Press, 1978.

Chatman, Seymour, ed. *Literary Style: A Symposium*. New York: Oxford University Press, 1971.

Christensen, Francis. *Notes for a New Rhetoric: Six Essays for Teachers*. New York: Harper & Row, 1967.

Clark, D. L. *Rhetoric in Greco-Roman Education*. New York: Columbia University Press, 1957.

Connors, Robert, Lisa Erde, and Andrea A. Lunsford, eds. *Classical Rhetoric and Modern Discourse: Essays in Honor of Edward P. J. Corbett*. Carbondale: Southern Illinois University Press, 1984.

Corbett, Edward P. J. *Classical Rhetoric for the Modern Student*, 2nd ed. New York: Oxford University Press, 1971.

————. "The Rhetoric of the Open Hand and the Rhetoric of the Closed Fist," *College Composition and Communication* 20 (December 1969): 288–296.

Corbett, Edward P. J., ed. *Rhetorical Analyses of Literary Works*. New York: Oxford University Press, 1969.

D'Angelo, Frank. *A Conceptual Theory of Rhetoric*. Cambridge, MA: Winthrop Publishing Co., 1975.

Dixon, Peter. *Rhetoric*, The Critical Idiom Series. London: Methuen, 1971.

Ehninger, Douglas, ed. *Contemporary Rhetoric: A Reader's Coursebook*. Glenview, IL: Scott, Foresman, 1972.

Ellul, Jacques. *Propaganda: The Formation of Men's Attitudes*, trs. Konrad Kellen and Jean Lemer. 1965; reprinted, New York: Vintage, 1973.

Fenelon, François de la Monthe. *Fenelon's Dialogues on Eloquence*, trs. Wilbur S. Howell. Princeton: Princeton University Press, 1951.

Freedom, Aviva, and Ian Pringle, eds. *Reinventing the Rhetorical Tradition*. Conway, AR: L & S Books/Canadian Council of Teachers of English, 1980.

Gibson, Walker. *Tough, Sweet, and Stuffy: An Essay on Modern American Prose Styles*. Bloomington: Indiana University Press, 1966.

Harrington, Elbert W. *Rhetoric and the Scientific Method of Inquiry: A Study of Invention*. Boulder: University of Colorado Press, 1948.

Horner, Winifred Bryan, ed. *Historical Rhetoric: An Annotated Bibliography of Selected Sources in English.* Boston: G. K. Hall, 1980.

————., ed. *The Present State of Scholarship in Historical and Contemporary Rhetoric.* Columbia, MO: University of Missouri Press, 1983.

Howell, Wilbur Samuel. *Eighteenth Century British Logic and Rhetoric.* Princeton: Princeton University Press, 1971.

————. *Logic and Rhetoric in England 1500–1700.* Princeton: Princeton University Press, 1956.

Howes, R. F., ed. *Historical Studies of Rhetoric and Rhetoricians.* Ithaca: Cornell University Press, 1961.

Joos, Martin. *The Five Clocks.* New York: Harcourt, Brace, World, 1967.

Kennedy, George. *The Art of Persuasion in Greece.* Princeton: Princeton University Press, 1963.

————. *The Art of Rhetoric in the Roman World.* Princeton: Princeton University Press, 1972.

Kinneavy, James L. *A Theory of Discourse.* Englewood Cliffs, NJ: Prentice-Hall, 1971.

Klaus, Carl H., ed. *Style in English Prose.* New York: Macmillan, 1968.

Kuhn, Thomas. *The Structure of Scientific Revolutions,* 2nd ed. Chicago: Chicago University Press, 1970.

Love, Glen A., and Michael Payne, eds. *Contemporary Essays on Style: Rhetoric, Linguistics, and Criticism.* Glenview: Scott, Foresman, and Co., 1969.

Martin, Harold C., Richard M. Ohmann, and James H. Wheatley. *The Logic and Rhetoric of Exposition,* 3rd ed. New York: Holt, Rinehart, Winston, 1969.

McKerrow, Ray E., ed. *Explorations in Rhetoric: Studies in Honor of Douglas Ehninger.* Glenview: Scott, Foresman & Co., 1984.

Miller, Joseph, Michael H. Prosser, and Thomas W. Benson. *Readings in Medieval Rhetoric.* Bloomington: Indiana University Press, 1973.

Mueller, Claus. *The Politics of Communication.* New York: Oxford University Press, 1973.

Murphy, James J., ed. *The Rhetorical Tradition and Modern Writing.* New York: The Modern Language Association, 1982.

Nichols, Marie Hochmuth. *Rhetoric and Criticism.* Baton Rouge: Louisiana State University Press, 1963.

Nilsen, Thomas R., ed. *Essays on Rhetorical Criticism.* New York: Random House, 1968.

Ong, Walter J., S. J. *Interfaces of the Word.* Ithaca: Cornell University Press, 1977.

————. *Presence of the Word.* Minneapolis: University of Minnesota Press, 1967.

————. *Rhetoric, Romance, and Technology: Studies in the Interaction of*

*Expression and Culture.* Ithaca: Cornell University Press, 1971.

Perelman, Chaim, and L. Olbrechts-Tyeca. *The New Rhetoric: A Treatise in Argumentation,* tr. John Wilkinson. Notre Dame: University of Notre Dame Press, 1969.

Richards, I. A. *The Philosophy of Rhetoric.* London: Oxford University Press, 1936.

Rockas, Leo. *Modes of Rhetoric.* New York: St. Martin's Press, 1964.

Schwartz, Joseph, and John R. Rycenga, eds. *The Province of Rhetoric.* New York: Ronald Press, 1965.

Shaughnessy, Mina. *Errors and Expectations.* New York: Oxford University Press, 1977.

Tanner, William E., and J. Dean Bishop, eds. *Rhetoric and Change.* Mesquite, TX: Ide House, 1982.

Vygotsky, Lem. *Thought and Language.* Cambridge, MA: MIT Press, 1962.

Weaver, Richard M. *The Ethics of Rhetoric.* Chicago: University of Chicago Press, 1953.

Winterowd, W. Ross, ed. *Contemporary Rhetoric: A Conceptual Background with Readings.* New York: Harcourt, Brace, Jovanovich, 1975.

———. *Rhetoric: A Synthesis.* New York: Holt, Rinehart, Winston, 1968.

Woodson, Linda. *A Handbook of Modern Rhetorical Terms.* Urbana, IL: National Council of Teachers of English, 1979.

# Index

## About the Author

ROBERT L. ROOT, JR., is Professor of English at Central Michigan University. He is the author of *Thomas Southerne* and has published articles in the *Journal of Popular Culture, Television and Teaching English*, and *Reinventing the Rhetorical Tradition*.